DIGITAL MARKETING ROADMAP

❧

LAUNCH AND GROW YOUR BUSINESS ON A BUDGET IN AN UNCERTAIN MARKET

CAMERON BANKS

DIGITAL MARKETING ROADMAP

BY CAMERON BANKS

PUBLISHED BY **SYNAST PUBLISHING**

ISBN:978-1-968418-11-3

INTRODUCTION

In today's rapidly evolving digital landscape, businesses face unprecedented challenges and opportunities. The uncertainty of the market, coupled with budget constraints, demands an innovative approach to marketing strategies. "Digital Marketing Roadmap" serves as a crucial guide for entrepreneurs and small business owners who aim to navigate this complex environment effectively. This book provides practical insights and actionable strategies to launch and grow a business without the need for extensive financial resources.

The digital marketing arena is vast and dynamic, often overwhelming for those unfamiliar with its intricacies. However, this guide breaks down the complexities into manageable steps, ensuring that readers can grasp the essentials of digital marketing and apply them to their unique business contexts. Whether it's understanding the nuances of social media platforms, leveraging search engine optimization, or crafting compelling content that resonates with target audiences, this book offers a comprehensive toolkit for success.

One of the core principles emphasized is the importance of adaptability. As consumer behaviors and technological advancements continue to shift, businesses must remain agile and responsive. This book highlights case studies and real-world examples that illustrate how businesses have thrived by embracing change and adopting innovative marketing techniques. By focusing on strategic planning and resourceful execution, readers will learn how to maximize their impact in the digital realm.

Furthermore, "Digital Marketing Roadmap" underscores the significance of analytics and data-driven decision-making. In an age where data is abundant, understanding how to interpret and utilize this information is crucial for optimizing marketing efforts and achieving sustainable growth. Through clear explanations and expert advice, this book equips readers with the knowledge needed to make informed decisions and track their progress effectively.

Ultimately, this guide is not just about surviving in an uncertain market but thriving by harnessing the power of digital marketing. With the right strategies and mindset, businesses can not only overcome challenges but also seize new opportunities for expansion and success.

CONTENTS

CHAPTER 1

INTRODUCTION TO DIGITAL MARKETING

Understanding the Basics

Online marketing is a complex field that has become a foundation unit for any firm that applies it in order to maximize its reach to the many people in the digital era. Digital marketing means the strategies and implementations that have been put in place in order to reach a wide range of audiences using digital media. Such channels are search engines, social media, emails, and websites, all of which have their settings for approaching new customers.

Knowledge of the digital landscape is one of the key constituents of digital marketing. This would mean identifying the different types of platforms and audiences that get attracted to them. An illustration of this would be the fact that younger audiences widely use Instagram and TikTok, whereas professional and business users mostly use LinkedIn. The above demographic understanding can enable a marketer to direct his or her marketing strategies in a manner that enables them to reach the target audience and appeal to them successfully.

The other important consideration is the formulation of an elaborate digital marketing plan. The main premise underlying this strategy should be the proper understanding of the goals and objectives of the brand. If you desire to raise brand awareness, encourage people to visit a particular website, or sell some product or service, it is highly desirable to have a clear plan. This strategy is supposed to specify the particular techniques that would be implemented, the means that would be used, and the method of gauging success.

Search engine optimization (SEO) is a major element of online marketing. Search engine optimization can enable a business to enhance visibility and placement of the business on search results pages. It includes the introduction of relevant keywords, quality content, backlinks, and so forth that help to obtain a better position in the search engine and, as a result, raise organic traffic.

Another crucial aspect is social media marketing, which allows businesses to communicate with their audience more personally and interactively. Brands through social media will be able to post content, respond to customer questions, and collect feedback, thereby creating a level of community and constructive loyalty amongst their followers.

The old email is still a potent marketing strategy for contacting customers. With the building of specific email campaigns, a business will be able to connect with the audience in a more personalized manner, providing personalized content, sales, and news that will interest the receiver and meet his or her wants.

Digital marketing also comprises content marketing. Here, it uses the concept of content creation and sharing in order to grow and maintain a static audience. Such material may be of many different forms, such as a blog post, video, infographic, and so on. This is aimed at adding value to the audience, which in turn makes the brand the source of authority in the field.

Measuring the effectiveness of digital marketing efforts requires comprehension of analytics and data. Businesses may understand what is effective and what needs to be enhanced by the analysis of such indicators as the traffic to the site, conversion rates, and engagement levels. This will enable the constant refinement of the marketing strategy in order to get improved outcomes.

The concept of digital marketing can be summed up as utilizing the capabilities of digital platforms to establish meaningful relationships with consumers. Through learning the fundamentals, companies will be able to formulate powerful points that will not only reach but also touch the hearts of their intended market to guarantee improvement and achievement in the digital environment.

Evolution of Digital Platforms

Digital platforms have transformed immensely in the past few decades. When they first appeared, online platforms were just an easy way to communicate and share simple information. Since then, however, due to technological changes, these platforms have developed into complicated environments that support a wide range of activities, including commerce, entertainment, social networking, and education.

During the initial times, platforms like email and simple websites ruled the digital world. They were mainly text-based platforms with minimal interactions. With the advancement of internet technology, multimedia integration of the internet through the employment of graphics and videos led to increased levels of usage and content enrichment. This change became the starting point of a more interactive digital space.

The emergence of social media sites such as Facebook, Twitter, and Instagram proved to be the turning point in the development of digital platforms. These sites brought a social transformation in the mood of people and produced virtual communities, where members exchanged their experiences, opinions, and content in real-time. Such features as live streaming, stories, and direct messaging have also been added to improve the interaction and engagement of the user further.

It is also seen that the evolution of e-commerce sites has been remarkable. They have shifted from mere online catalogs to high-tech online shops with individualized shopping, safe and trouble-free payment systems, and streamlined logistics. Amazon and platforms such as Alibaba have changed the game of online shopping by providing an extensive list of products and services to choose from at the press of a button.

Mobile technology has also enhanced the process of creating digital platforms. Due to the ubiquity of smartphones and other tablets, platforms needed to be scaled down to support the smaller (usually touch-enabled) screens. The result of the shift has been the design of mobile-first platforms where the focus is on the user experience on the mobile platform. Apps have emerged as a dominant platform with tight integration of device capabilities with GPS, camera, and sensors.

The development of cloud computing can also be regarded as another huge step in the development of digital platforms. The solutions provided by cloud-based platforms possess flexibility and scalability, thus letting businesses provide services that any corner of the world can access. This has simplified the development of Software as a Service (SaaS), allowing customers to subscribe to software applications that are hosted on distant servers.

The introduction of artificial intelligence (AI) and machine learning in digital platforms has presented new opportunities for personalizing and automating digital platforms. The algorithms based on AI will be capable of studying the way that a user acts and their preferences in order to provide them with adjusted content and suggestions. Such a degree of personalization increases both user satisfaction and engagement, and thus platforms become more efficient in addressing the needs of users.

Concerns of privacy and information protection have come into the limelight as digital systems have undergone various changes. The sheer volume of information produced by the users requires a strong security level to safeguard confidential data. Social networking sites have now started to use high-end encryption and privacy mechanisms to guarantee user confidence and adherence to the rules.

To sum up, the evolution of digital platforms shows the high level of technological innovation and user expectations. Whether through basic communication aids to multiple, multi-purpose ecosystems, digital platforms have become a critical part of contemporary society, providing varied possibilities in terms of networking, business, and creativity.

Key Terminologies

When it comes to digital marketing, it is important to develop an understanding of the lingo of the field, as it allows for effective planning and a strategy. This chapter will explore the required terminologies that constitute the core of digital marketing to shed light on what they mean and how they are employed.

Search Engine Optimization (SEO) is at the center stage of digital marketing. It is a term used to denote the act of increasing the visibility of a website in the search engine results pages (SERP). SEO can be used to enhance the organic traffic flowing into a website through multiple methods like keyword optimization, backlinking, and content creation.

The other milestone term is Pay-Per-Click (PPC) advertising. PPC is a type of internet promotion, during which the advertiser pays a fee whenever their ad is clicked. It involves the purchase of visits to the site, as opposed to the effort to obtain such visits naturally. One of the most common locations of PPC advertisements is Google Ads.

Content marketing refers to a marketing strategy aimed at the creation, publication, and dissemination of information of value that is relevant and consistent with other principles. This strategy is aimed at the attraction and retention of a well-defined audience. The end of the line is motivated by profitable customer action. This includes the development of blogs, videos, infographics, and other content that communicate and inspire the viewer.

Marketing in social media refers to the use of social sites such as Facebook, Instagram, Twitter, and LinkedIn with the aim of marketing products and services. The benefit of this kind of marketing is that not only does it increase brand awareness, but it also enables a direct engagement of customers, creating a community around a brand.

In digital marketing, it is no secret that email marketing is still a very strong tool, and its characteristics consist of sending commercial messages to a group of people via email. It is a very efficient manner of cultivating leads, customer information, and marketing products or services.

Analytics is a significant element of digital marketing, as it entails obtaining, quantifying, and analysing statistics in order to realise consumer patterns and enhance promotional initiatives. Such tools as Google Analytics give information about the traffic of a site, user activity, and conversion rates.

Conversion Rate Optimization (CRO) involves the optimization of the proportion of visitors to websites who perform a target action, e.g., purchasing or subscribing to a newsletter. This is done by A/B tests, user comments, and other methods that improve the user experience.

In digital marketing, it is key to know the customer journey. It is a term that is used to describe the ultimate whole experience by customers when dealing with a brand, including what they go through from the brand's initial start-up to the stage of purchase and even after the purchase. Customer journey mapping helps marketers find the touchpoints and maximize user experience at each stop.

Influencer marketing is a strategy that entails the use of people with a large following on social media platforms to market products or services. The rationale for this strategy is to use the trust and authority established by the influencers among their audience to achieve brand awareness and sales.

Lastly, mobile marketing has become a famous concept due to the widespread use of smartphones. This will be achieved by targeting the consumers via mobile phones through SMS messages, mobile applications, and responsive websites, to make sure the marketing campaigns are available on mobile devices, irrespective of where the consumer might be.

The all-important terminologies are the blocks that define digital marketing and offer it a universal lingo to aid communication among its workforce. These terms and concepts are very important types of knowledge that must be mastered by anybody who seeks to succeed in the digital world.

Digital vs Traditional Marketing

Digital marketing and traditional marketing are the two contrasting strategies that are the cornerstones in the realm of marketing, when considering how businesses can reach out to their clients. Every approach is accompanied by its strategies, instruments, and philosophies with unique advantages and difficulties. These two strategies, although frequently believed to resemble each other, can be combined to create a complete overview of effective marketing in the case of a specific strategy.

The name of traditional marketing is the old trick; it comprises various offline activities such as television, radio, print, direct mail, and so on. This type of marketing is based on getting in touch with a wide audience with the help of mass media. The touchy character of print media and the aural or visual connection of TV and radio stations make a concrete relationship with the consumers. It is commonly perceived that traditional marketing is more personal because it can physically reach potential customers and present them with a sensory experience that cannot be delivered through digital media.

Nevertheless, conventional marketing is characterised by limitations, which are largely related to its measurability and cost-efficiency. Measuring the success of a print advertisement or a television advert may prove difficult to match since it may be based on indirect means, like the survey of the customer or the sales figures. Moreover, conventional marketing may sometimes demand a considerable amount of investment, which is not always possible in smaller companies with low funds at their disposal.

Conversely, digital marketing has become a determinant, whereby the internet has been harnessed to reach the consumers. This technique covers many strategies, including search engine optimization (SEO), marketing content, social media campaigns, and email marketing. A key factor that has contributed to the success of digital marketing is the fact that they have allowed marketers to target a certain demographic accurately, with the potential to track and measure campaign success in a real-time setting. This data-oriented practice enables companies to change the tactics in a minimum time frame, stretching the profit margin to the maximum.

Digital marketing has a wide coverage, crosses geographical boundaries, and can make a business reach the rest of the world. Social media, especially, has transformed the brand-consumer relationship, leading to a direct interaction between the brands and the consumers. Digital marketing is interactive, and this is conversational and improves the relationship between the customers as it builds brand loyalty.

However, inasmuch as digital marketing is beneficial, it has its challenges. The digital environment is dynamic, and changes are occurring all the time; marketers have to be familiar with the current trends in the industry and the available technology. Moreover, the amount of content accessible online is huge, and this factor can become an obstacle to the recognition of brands; this is why it is vital to employ imaginative and innovative techniques in order to attract consumers.

One of the conundrums that arises over digital and traditional marketing is which one is effective. Nevertheless, the most effective promotion campaigns usually combine both tactics, using the advantages of each and combining them into a complementary one. The traditional method can be used to create brand awareness and credibility, whereas the digital forms can be used to encourage action and conversion.

In summary, it can be said that the final decision between digital and traditional marketing must be dictated by the exact target of the business, its audience, and the resources available to it. Comprehending the peculiarities of both methods, businesses can develop a customized promotion strategy that will capitalize on the virtues of both online and offline segments, involving a wide range of audiences and effective outcomes. As marketing conditions change further, this combination of the two modes will also be more significant, and it can become a well-balanced and broad approach to deliver and attract consumers in the contemporary era.

CHAPTER 2

BUILDING A DIGITAL MARKETING STRATEGY

Setting Goals and Objectives

The goals and objectives of digital marketing are the core of the entire marketing tactic, and having them clarified and defined will help the strategy to be appreciated. These aspects act as the light that will guide the whole marketing program, so that all the activities carried out are in accordance with the big picture of the business. Goal and objective setting cannot be administrative; it involves strategy and requires careful thought and wisdom.

Specificity holds the core of setting effective goals. Generalities like raising brand awareness or generating more sales do not give a clear guide on the way to act. Goals should instead be communicated in a stereotype. An example could be to achieve an increase in the traffic on the website by 20 percent within the next six months, and that alone provides what success should be and when it should be reached. This degree of particularity makes abstract concepts easily applicable by making them realizable goals, and hence, they can be pursued in an orderly manner.

The same can be said about the measurability of goals. In the world of digital marketing, where numbers are king, measuring success is the priority. The measurable objectives help the marketers monitor the progress, determine the effectiveness of the strategies, and act accordingly with the help of specific data. This data-driven method not only boosts accountability but also gives the flexibility to shift gears when it comes to the strategies to adopt due to an emerging trend or sudden challenges.

Another important issue is the relevance of the goals to the general business strategy. Aims have to accommodate the larger goals of the organization, where the digital marketing activity should play a significant role in the success and growing capacity of the company. Such an alignment promotes similarity among departments and instills uniformity in pursuit of business goals.

Goals that are time-bound are really necessary to continue serving as momentum and focus. Deadlines induce a sense of urgency, which drives the team toward a goal, as set by the marketers. Such time frames put an end to procrastination and provide smooth progress toward the intended results. Furthermore, time-based objectives enable the strategies to be reviewed at stipulated periods to ensure that interventions and amendments are made on time.

The same kind of rigor must be followed in goal setting. Objectives transmit large goals into workable actions, thus allowing clear pursuit of attaining goals. They are the blueprint of operations where particular activities are spelled out to attain the goals being pursued. Such a statement leads to well-built objectives that satisfy the SMART standards of being specific, measurable, achievable, relevant, and time-bound.

Establishing goals and objectives is a cyclical process. The digital environment is changing, and strategies must be used to traverse it. The frequent overview and change of goals ensures that these goals correspond to the existing trends and priorities of the organization. The dynamic strategy provides a possibility to include new knowledge and technologies and to update the marketing strategy effectively.

In the bottom line, goal and objective setting is simply developing a clear vision of what is to be attained in the future, and describing the pathways that should be traversed in achieving the desired vision. It is an essential part of strategic planning, which offers guidance and motivation required to move in the non-inhibiting landscape of digital marketing. Having clear goals and objectives, businesses can better capitalize on the use of digital channels to grow and become long-term, successful players in the ever-evolving market.

Identifying Target Audience

The knowledge of your target market is the key component of an effective digital marketing plan. It is not only important to know the demographics, but also to go further and learn more and more about the psychographics and behavioral tendencies that characterize your prospective customers. In identifying a target audience, one must be sensitive to considering a number of variables that have a bearing on consumer choices.

This is preceded by thorough market research. It entails the collection of information through different channels like surveys, focus groups, and social media analytics. Such tools will help you to understand the preferences, the needs, and the challenges of your audience. It is crucial to divide your audience by these findings to make more personal marketing strategies. The segmentation can be done with respect to their age, gender, income, lifestyle, or even their purchasing behavior.

A good strategy to know the audience is to map buyer personas. They are quasi-fictional characters who act as representations of your ideal customers. An effective persona has described details such as the demographic factors, personal interests, work experience, and his/her purchase patterns. Furthermore, by imagining what your ideal customer looks like, you may provide them with marketing messages that speak to them more specifically regarding their needs and wants.

The other important point is the investigation of customer feedback and reviews. This type of feedback offers first-hand information about what the customers like or do not like concerning your products or services. It helps to emphasize areas that need to be improved and can be used to dictate the product development and marketing strategies. Reach out to your client by commenting and reviewing, which will also earn you the virtue of trust and loyalty since the customers will be made to feel that their opinion means something to you.

Social platforms cannot be underrated when it comes to knowing the audience behaviour. In doing so, you can collect information about its engagement, the most active hours, and the type of content that gets the most attention. Social media tools such as Facebook Insights and Twitter Analytics have more detailed reports to present about demographic and engagement data of the audience.

You will also have to monitor your competitors. Segmenting the audience will inform them of the available gaps and opportunities in the market. You may use such tools as SEMrush or Ahrefs to get an idea of what keywords your competitors use and how people read their content.

More so, with the development of new technologies like artificial intelligence and machine learning, the analysis of the audience became a revolution. These technologies may handle massive amounts of data to establish tendencies and consumer patterns and target and customize them more diversely.

Lastly, keep in mind that you should revisit and update your knowledge of the target audience more often. Consumer preferences and behavior are forever changing based on cultural changes, economic changes, and technology. This helps you to continue engaging and converting your audience. You will be able to change your marketing strategies to fit the new needs of your audience because you are up to date.

Basically, target audience identification is a continuous process that involves commitment and change of pace. When you know more about them, your audience, and how they forge their motivations, you will be able to craft more constructive marketing campaigns that can not only reach but also appeal to your target audience.

Budgeting and Resources

When it comes to digital marketing, budgeting and the setting aside of resources are key factors with regard to how far a given marketing campaign will go. The process of budget making is a detailed examination of different financial factors so that no dollar goes to waste; instead, all of them are part of the big picture of the marketing plan. Budgeting for digital marketing is not limited to the sum of money; it involves the prediction of returns as well as control of expenses to maximize effectiveness.

The most important thing about budgeting is the realization of the marketing objective. The existence of clear and measurable objectives helps to decide what resources are to be concentrated in the various streams and projects. At the popularity of the brand, the traffic on the site, or sales promotion, every goal requires its own, individually requested financial strategy that could support the anticipated expectations.

Strategic budgeting is the process that implies a thorough assessment of previous campaign experience. Evaluation of the past information provides marketers with trends, achievements, and points to develop. Such hindsight is worth a gold mine when it comes to foretelling future trends and making valuable decisions concerning where to invest resources efficiently. In addition, budget plans can also be enhanced with the help of analytics tools that will give real-time reports on consumer behaviour and campaign results.

Digital marketing resources are not defined only by money. Technological tools and other personnel (human resources) are also very essential in the planning process, and they also need to be planned carefully. It is necessary to attract a team of professionals who could perform the marketing strategy. This goes beyond recruiting the talent and must also involve long-term investment in training and development in order to stay abreast of the fast-changing digital environment.

Technology is significant in the current advertisements. By investing in more sophisticated tools and a platform that would help to automate, analyze data, and connect with the customers, the efficiency and effectiveness of the marketing operations could be significantly boosted. Whether it could be using customer relationship management (CRM) systems, social media management tools, and even tax software, it pays off to invest in the appropriate technology with regard to increased productivity and output.

The other important part of resource planning is time management. Project management is effective in making sure that all the marketing activities are carried out within the stipulated time without fear of running out of budget, and on-time results are delivered. The application of the project management software would facilitate monitoring achievements, organizing the work, and synchronizing group activity.

Contingencies are also considered in a well-organized budget. Digital marketing is dynamic, so it is possible to disregard the challenges and opportunities that can appear unexpectedly. Saving a small amount of the budget on such eventualities gives the marketers time to adjust quickly without having to cancel the whole product campaign.

Finally, budgeting and resource allocation are two key components of digital marketing, and the success of these depends on flexibility and adaptability. With the changes in market conditions and the preferences taken by the consumers, marketers need to be in a position to re-strategize and refocus on resources to remain competitive. Frequent reviews and updates of the budget plans will help to ensure that the undertaken marketing is consistent with the existing business goals and the business realities.

By ensuring realistic and goal-oriented budgeting and resource management, digital marketing programs can reach maximum efficiency and effectiveness, which will provide growth and measurable results. This is the strategic planning of monetary and non-monetary resources that are the main pillars of an effective digital marketing roadmap that will help businesses to reach a sustainability level of and success in the digital world.

Monitoring and Evaluation

Another important step in all effective digital marketing strategies is the continuous monitoring and evaluation process. The stage entails a comprehensive record of the success of the marketing campaigns, processing of the information gathered, and decisions made on how to do it better in the future. The first aim would be to make sure that the marketing programs are in line with the targeted intentions and provide the desired results.

Firstly, you need to set properly measurable and meaningful key performance indicators (KPI), which reflect the goals of the campaign. These KPIs will be used to determine a reference point through which the efficiency of the marketing can be measured. KPIs used in internet marketing encompass the number of guests to websites, the conversion rates, clicks, and the degree of customer interaction. The establishment of these indicators allows the marketers to have a quantitative idea of whether their strategies are performing well.

The following step is a collection and analysis of the information with the help of the different analytical tools and technologies. The behavior of customers and the success of campaigns can be well described using tools or sources like Google Analytics, social media insights, and customer relationship management (CRM) dashboards. The tools assist in terminating trends, determining the wishes of the audience, and identifying areas that should be tackled better.

When you have all the data, it is important to analyze the results so as to reach relevant conclusions. It involves comparing the results realized with the predetermined KPIs and obtaining the differences. In this way, a marketer will be able to decide what parts of the campaign have been performing well and those that have to be changed. As an example, when a conversion rate of a campaign turns out to be lower than it should be, it could mean that it is necessary to either optimize the call-to-action or enhance the user experience on the landing page.

In addition, the lessons obtained through monitoring and evaluation help the marketers make data-oriented decisions. These choices may be reshaping the allocation of resources to more effective means of transmission, changing the message to make it highly relevant to the target market, or testing new strategies to improve performance. This process is an iterative process that helps to render the marketing strategy dynamic and one that is in tune with the market situation.

Monitoring and evaluation are also essential during strategic planning, besides optimizing the campaigns that are taking place. Marketers are in a position to create future trends through analyzing past performance. It gives potential for developing more effective marketing strategies that are more suited to the expected behaviors and preferences of consumers.

Moreover, good monitoring and evaluation create accountability for the marketing team. Through frequent monitoring of the performance statistics, team members are able to know more about their roles and their contribution to the entire strategy. This openness will further promote a culture of constantly improving and working in teams, as coworkers will help each other in order to reach shared objectives.

In total, the monitoring and evaluation process is inevitably needed in the domain of digital marketing. It gives insights to improve the strategies, boost performance, and promote growth in the long term. With continuous tracking and research of campaign performance, marketers will be in a position to ensure that their efforts are relevant to business goals and will still add value to the business.

CHAPTER 3

SEARCH ENGINE OPTIMIZATION

Keyword Research

Within the context of digital marketing, keyword research may be aptly described as one of the fundamental components that spur the success of online campaigns. It entails recognizing and studying the words that individuals type in search engines to give the marketer ideas of the interests and requirements of customers. The findings of this research are not just limited to finding common words or phrases, but also connect them with the intention of the search and their compatibility with the products or services being provided.

The first process undertaken in the keyword research process is a brainstorming activity about potential keywords that are useful to the business or niche. It could be done by applying the practice of walking in the shoes of the target audience to think of what they would look like when seeking the products or services that are provided. It is also essential to ponder broadly and take into consideration variations, synonyms, and comparable terms that probable consumers will capitalize.

After having the list of possible keywords, the second stage is to evaluate the number of competitors and the search volume of these keywords. There is quite a range of resources that can help marketers in this kind of analysis and can offer data concerning the searching frequency of specific terms and their rank difficulty. Such analysis is useful in ranking keywords with high search volumes and relatively low competition, and thus makes it easier to rank well in the search engine results.

The second essential thing in keyword research is the interpretation of the purpose of keywords. One can classify search intent into informational, navigational, and transactional. Informational intent means that the user is searching, navigational intent implies that the user searches a distinct website, and transactional intent means that the user is willing to buy something. The purpose is to match the impression with the requisites of the user, and the content shall determine how well a well-managed marketing strategy can serve to grip the various phases of the buyer journey.

Moreover, in keyword research, long-tail keywords matter more, and they are presented as longer and more specific keywords or phrases. Though they might get lesser search volumes, they are usually more converting due to targeting users who are at later stages of buying. As an example, a visitor who queries for the best running shoes with flat feet will be more likely to buy one than a visitor who queries for running shoes.

Keyboard research is more than just having the right keywords when a digital marketing strategy is incorporated. It also involves finding ways of naturally inserting these keywords in website content, meta descriptions, and titles, among other aspects of a page, to enable it to be optimized in terms of search engines. This not only increases search engine ranking but also boosts user experience as he or she is shown relevant content that fits the expectations of the search query.

It is also important to monitor/refresh the keywords strategy when its search integration and user behavior change. Relying on regular updates to keyword research guarantees a consistent marketing strategy that stays closely connected with the latest trends and, hence, will help attract the target audience. Digital marketing success will depend on this adjustment and optimization process on a regular basis.

Finally, keyword research is an ever-changing process that can be the foundation of digital marketing activities. Once you know what potential customers are shopping around with and match your marketing strategies to the same, you increase your online presence, bring the right traffic to your site, and attain your marketing goals.

On-Page SEO Techniques

It is crucially important to make sure that a certain site gets noticed in the enormous online realm. On-page search engine optimization as an element of digital marketing is vital in improving the visibility and user activity of a website. This method concentrates on optimizing single web pages so as to rank high and receive more traffic from search engines. With the careful optimization of a webpage, on-page SEO helps search engines and their users to interpret the content and the context easily.

Keywords play a very important part in the whole process of on-page SEO. These are the keywords and phrases that users use in search engines to seek information. With the proper study of keywords, the marketer will be able to find the keywords that are pertinent and high-traffic related to their niche. After coming up with these keywords, they should be naturally introduced into different sections of the webpage, such as the title, the headings, and throughout the text body. Nevertheless, naturally using keywords and not identifying keyword stuffing are required to be kept in mind so as to avoid search engine penalties.

One more important thing is the optimization of meta tags, meta title, and meta description. The meta title, which is usually the initial idea that clients will get about a search outcome, ought to be brief, descriptive, and include the main keyword. Likewise, the meta description must be short enough to summarize their content, and in addition, it must provoke the users to visit the site by clicking on it. Such factors not only affect the click-throughs but also offer the search engines some contextual information with regard to the page.

A key value of successful on-page SEO is content quality. Informative, useful, original, high-quality content is more likely to provide a backlink, which plays a critical role in terms of SEO. Moreover, content must be set out using suitable headings and subheadings to make it more readable and allow easy access for users as well as the search engines. Subsequently, the user experience can also be improved by introducing multimedia elements such as images, videos, and infographics. Still, they are expected to be fast-loading and include explanatory alt text.

Another very important factor is user experience. The design and framework of the site should be user-friendly so that a visitor will experience no difficulties in using and locating the information that he/she is interested in. This means that they must be responsive so that they can be viewed on different devices and all screen sizes, and they should also have a quick loading time so that the user will not feel frustrated. Internal linking is also of benefit since users can work through the related content, and search engines will indicate the relevance and usefulness of the various pages on the site.

On-page SEO also includes technical details such as URL structure and mobile-friendliness. They should be user- and search engine-friendly because of the descriptive, clean, and relevant keywords in the URLs. As mobile devices become more and more frequently used, it is no longer an option to make sure that the site is mobile-friendly, but a requirement. The mobile-optimized site will not only deliver on the user experience, but the search engines will also prefer the site for ranking.

Through these factors, the on-page SEO methods will play a critical role in promoting the position of a site in search engine ranking, resulting in visibility, traffic, and finally, conversions. Keeping updated and in the loop with the latest on-page SEO recommendations is an essential component in the constantly changing environment of digital marketing.

Off-Page SEO Strategies

In digital marketing, Off-Page SEO tactics play a critical role in the online positioning and credibility of a web page. Off-page SEO is not within the site, similar to on-page SEO, and the activities referred to as off-page apply themselves principally to the external factors of a site and increasing the dread and respect of a site. The plans play crucial roles in establishing a series of quality backlinks, visibility of the brand, and development of relationships that can aid the performance of the site in the search rankings.

The backlink is at the heart of off-page SEO since it is the link that comes from an outside source to the site. These backlinks serve as a testimonial of sorts that search engines know that the contents are valid and worthwhile. The quality and quantity of the backlinks are important; the links of reputable sites have priority, and they can play an important role in making the site authoritative. Some indicate that their strategies to get such links are guest blogging or writing content that is posted on another website and outreach, meaning building contacts with other web admins and influencers so that they can be persuaded to place a link to that site.

The usage of social media is another successful off-page strategy. Businesses can also reach out to more people and influence their brand through an active presence on social media. Although the use of social media has no direct effect on SEO ranking, it is important in enhancing traffic flow to the site and making the brand well-known to others. Interesting posts on social media sites can catch the attention of visitors who may later refer to the site or even post the content on other sites, which influences the impact of the site on SEO on a secondary level.

Off-page SEO also has potential in online forums and communities. A business can position itself as an expert in its industry by sharing useful information and knowledge in suitable forums. This not only helps in making the brand be considered but also helps in attracting the members of the forum to even go to the website to get more information, which may result in the development of backlinks. However, it is also important that the contributions are not too commercial but rather focused on the actual values, as later on it may cause negative images as well as fines on the part of the search engines.

Another off-page strategy that is very effective is influencer marketing. Influencers have a strong following in a specific niche; therefore, by designing collaborations with those individuals, businesses can reach out to new audiences and make them trustworthy. With the help of influencers, a brand can be presented to new users, who will be willing to provide the brand with natural backlinks and promote it through word-of-mouth. This plan is deeply built on the identification of the right influencers whose followers will fit the firm's target market.

Moreover, the off-page activities can be augmented by inputting and optimizing a Google My Business profile within local SEO practices. This profile is meant to make a business visible in the local search results, which puts it in front of potential customers within a given area. The reputation of the business online can be further improved by encouraging the satisfied customers to leave positive reviews on Google and other review sites.

The effects of off-page SEO strategies can be realized only after spending some time and effort, but the effects of ranking a site as well as its authority are undeniable. When paying attention to the establishment of strong groups of qualified backlinks, the interaction with the audience in the environment of social networks, engagement in communities in the environment of the network, utilizing mutually beneficial cooperation with influencers, and maximizing local representation, a business can increase its online presence tremendously. All these strategies will work towards an all-around SEO strategy that guarantees long-term visibility and success in the competitive web world.

SEO Tools and Analytics

This is to say that in the current swarming environment where digital marketing is taking place, it is necessary to use the appropriate tools and analytics to optimize the performance of the search engines. The portfolio of the digital marketer has been bombarded with loads of SEO tools that can be used to provide visibility, boost rankings, and eventually drive traffic to the sites. These tools include keyword research and on-page optimization through backlink analysis and competitor benchmarking.

Keyword research tools play critical roles in locating the appropriate words and phrases that prospective clients use to search for products or services. These are tools that enable one to identify keywords that are few but in volume and less competitive, as these are able to influence the position of a site in the search engine. Marketers can find out what their users are searching for, and while the user is doing this, it will be prudent to determine the need and provide content to match the demands, and this will enhance the chances of the marketers to appear in the searches.

On-page optimization tools also cannot be underrated since they help to improve the content and structure of a website, making it more pleasing to search engines. These tools scan different components like meta tags, headers, and content quality, giving their suggestions on ways to improve. Making sure that a site is very good on both the technical front and content is key to getting better search engine rankings.

Whether it is the quality or quantity of a link pointing to their site, backlink analysis tools equip the marketer with the advantage of monitoring and analyzing the same. As backlinks are the essential element of search engine algorithms, the information about the backlink profile may be used to elaborate on the strategies that can be employed to create high-quality links. Marketers can also use these tools to detect and disavow the harmful or spammy links that may have a negative impact on search engine ranking.

Competitor benchmarking tools provide information on the strategies that rival firms use. Another way is using the keywords, backlinking, and content strategies of your competitors as a source where marketers will find opportunities to enhance their SEO strategies. The insights can be translated to devise better campaigns that leverage the competitor weaknesses and market gaps.

Analytics is also included in the SEO process and provides data-based content that may be used in decision-making. Marketers can monitor the performance of the website and user actions, as well as conversion level, with the help of such tools as Google Analytics. With the help of this data, marketers will be able to extract trends, estimate the success of their SEO techniques, and make the necessary changes to improve performance.

In addition to that, reporting and visualization are made easier with the help of SEO tools and analytics. Detailed reports produced with the aid of these tools can be used to convey the effectiveness of SEO campaigns to vested parties. Through visualizations, data becomes clear and brief in that interpreting and taking the necessary action is simple.

Another reason for a unified approach is the incorporation of SEO-related tools with other marketing channels used on a digital platform. Marketers can determine the complete picture of their digital presence by integrating the information from their sources with SEO tools, including social media, email marketing, and many more. With this integration, there is a possibility of having a more strategic approach and implementation in the digital marketing activities, making sure that all their dimensions work together to promote the overall business objectives.

In the ever-changing online environment, many more tools and analytics are becoming important in maintaining a competitive advantage. Lifelong learning and adjustment must be undertaken to fully realize the potential of these tools, such that digital marketing would not fail as its effects would continually change to keep pace with the upgrades both in the search engines and with the user, too.

CHAPTER 4

CONTENT MARKETING ESSENTIALS

Creating Engaging Content

When it comes to digital marketing, one of the most important aspects of a successful strategy is to develop content that can attract the audience. The fundamentals of creating engaging content are that the audience gets drawn to it and their attention keeps them glued and open to engaging in it, therefore, creating a connection between the brand and the consumer. Creation of such content will involve some elements of creativity, insight, and a deep understanding of the intended audience.

First of all, it is important to target the audience. It entails getting used to their interests, likes, and practices. This knowledge aids in cutting down the content that appeals to them at a personal level. Being aware of their demographic background, age, gender, location, and even digital habits, one can considerably increase the relevance of the content. Not only does this attention-getter create trust and loyalty, but it also creates trust and loyalty over time.

After getting proper knowledge of the intended audience, the next thing to emphasize is the storytelling part. The art of creation in content creation is strong in storytelling. It has nothing to do with the transfer of information but with the spinning of stories that intertwine emotion and memorable experiences. A brand can be humanized through the stories so that it becomes closer and easier to access. They enable the brands to deliver their values and mission to the audience in a form that is interesting and effective.

Visual elements are quite important in engaging content, too. Data may be more attractive and easier to digest in the context of the digital environment, thanks to visualization. Since there is a range of graphics and visual material, including images and infographics, videos, and interactive features, such as quizzes and polls, the deck can be appealing to various audiences and types of learners. The trick here is that all visuals must have the same style and branding to support the identity of the brand.

In addition, the tone and voice of the writing are also essential factors. They would have to be in tandem with the brand personality and the taste of the audience. The brand voice can either be casual and friendly (or even relaxed) or formal and authoritative, but the consistency is essential. It aids in creating an acceptable and credible brand image.

The sharing platform is also another essential point. Each platform is more or less strong and has a different audience. For example, LinkedIn is more appropriate for posting more professional and detailed articles, whereas Instagram might be the best place to post visually based content. The key is to gain insights about the complexity of every platform in order to maximize the engagement of marketers within their content.

Interactivity also plays the role of making the content interesting. Inclusive techniques of audience participation, such as comments, shares, or self-created content, can go a long way to improve the participation. Interactive media has twice the same effect: increasing the duration of the user on a page and promoting the company because of shares and word-of-mouth.

Lastly, it is critical to measure the effectiveness of content. Keeping a check on factors like likes, shares, comments, and conversion rates using the tool of analytics can give important details on which is working and what is not. This kind of analytical process enables constant optimization and advancement with content strategies.

Basically, making compelling content is a very complex process that involves the integration of the creative and the insightful. The audience needs to understand it, it needs a good story, attractive pictures, and the same brand voice. Through the successful utilization of these components, the brands will be able to produce content that not only attracts the audience but also retains and converts them into their customers.

Content Distribution Channels

When it comes to digital marketing within a sea of opportunities, one could identify with a set of routes to travel; it is the same in content distribution, where the proper selection of avenues to cater to content is important. Every channel offers its distinct opportunities and challenges, which have to be comprehended to make the distribution of content effective. The distribution channels may greatly influence the success of the marketing campaigns, not only in this digital age where people have little time, but also where information is widely available.

Major players in the content distribution arena have been the social media sites. These social media platforms include Facebook, Instagram, Twitter, LinkedIn, and TikTok, with billions of users and have unsurpassed outreach and engagement potential. The platforms serve varying demographics with a diverse content type, and therefore, a marketer must ensure that his/her strategy fits the type of audience and platform requirements. As an example, Instagram offers a highly visual-based environment, i.e., it suits the brands that are able to tell their stories visually; meanwhile, LinkedIn has proved to be a great tool for B2B marketers that is used to reach other professionals.

Although younger channels have started to pop up, email is still a pillar in digital marketing approaches. This makes it an effective method to nurture leads and retain customers since it will send personal messages straight to the inbox of the audience. Effective email marketing begins with the art of creating interesting content that can connect to the readers and to gear it at the opportune timing, as well as segmentation to make it effective and appealing to the readers/audience.

The use of search engines like Google is central in the distribution of content in the form of search engine optimization (SEO). Businesses can stimulate traffic on their digital assets by making them appear on specific search queries through optimization. SEO is the ability to know all about the keywords, the intention behind the user, and the changes caused by the algorithm in order to keep their place in the eyes of the searchers and to be competitive. The quality of content at the top of the search engines not only increases the number of visitors but also establishes credit and influence in the market.

Another viable distribution option is content syndication, where the marketer can get the coverage and distribution of their content in collaboration with third-party sites. When posting the content on worthy sites, the business draws new audiences and improves its brand presence. This strategy will entail the proper selection of syndication partners so as not to lose brand values and audience interests.

Pay-per-click (PPC) and social media advertising have the benefit of concentrated exposure along with measurable results. Such media permit the marketer to target particular groups of the population through their demographics, interests, and online habits. This monitoring and assessment of advertisement performance brings useful knowledge of the campaign efficiency and the return on investment (ROI), on which the optimization can be done in a data-driven manner.

Online video innovations, such as YouTube and podcasting, have become popular media for the distribution of interesting content. The emergence of multimedia consumption behavior also demonstrates the need to diversify the format of content in order to suit the preferences of the audience. Podcasts present an exclusive means of reaching out to the audience with the help of storytelling and a thought leadership style. In contrast, video content can engage and educate both visually and audibly.

Finally, a profound knowledge of the target audience, a niche of content, and marketing goals should guide the choice of channels of content distribution. With the help of an adequate combination of channels, marketers are capable of maximizing the reach they possess and encouraging people to connect and interact in meaningful ways with the message. In this constantly changing online world, it is essential to be informed about new channels and new trends in order to achieve success long-term.

Measuring Content Success

The question, however, lying at the core of the digital marketing environment, changes at the pace at which the sphere develops, is whether the content is effective or not, and the answer, in such a case, can make or break a particular business. As important as knowing the number of likes or the number of shares, measuring content success is about thoroughly analyzing a set of metrics that can show how people perceive you and your brand, as well as a possible future outcome, known as a return on investment or ROI. This complex analysis has to have a strategic course that is aligned with the broad objectives of a marketing campaign.

First of all, it is important to specify clear goals. Depending on the direction, such as enhancing brand awareness, attracting leads, driving traffic on the websites, and improving customer engagement, each requires certain metrics to measure them. To give an example, in case brand awareness is the main goal, reach, impressions, and mentions on social media will be important metrics. Such indicators give an idea about the extent to which the content is spread and how widespread its exposure is to the target audience.

The benchmarks of engagement are a key to measuring the success of content. These are likes, comments, marks of sharing the content, and time spent by users on interacting with the content. It is also a sign of a good rate of engagement and one that shows that the content might connect well with the audience and that they want to engage and share it with their network. This voluntary self-verification multiplies the content and further boosts its credibility because individuals tend to be more convinced by suggestions made by their peers.

Conversion analysis is another important part of the information on the success of the content. These measures are especially critical to a campaign that aims to achieve a certain behavior, including subscribing to a newsletter, downloading a guide, or making a purchase. Some of the most important measures reflecting the degree to which content has allowed users to navigate through the decision-making process include conversion rates, click-through rate (CTR), and cost per conversion. Monitoring these metrics will help the marketers determine which content is most effective in converting interest to action.

Along with these quantitative indicators, it is also possible to mention such qualitative feedback. This is obtainable in the form of surveys, comments, and reviews, and it makes the perception and attitude of the audience with regard to the content clear. The information on the emotional and cognitive levels of the content assists in narrowing down future strategies in order to provide greater correspondence to the needs and expectations of the audience.

Moreover, measuring the success of content with the help of tools and technologies is also a part of the mix. Team or department performance can be tracked using analytic websites like Google Analytics or social media insights, as well as designated content analysis tools that capture comprehensive data, which can be used to make business decisions. The tools can be used to divide data by demographics, behavior, and other applicable parameters to provide a finer detail on how the audience interacts with them.

Lastly, the constantly changing landscape of digital marketing must also be subject to constant improvement. Conducting performance evaluations and analyses allows marketers to detect trends, streamline plans, and make data-based choices. Through successive optimization of content with the help of performance statistics, companies can make sure the promotion process is up to date and still sufficient to achieve the business goals.

Essentially, the evaluation of content success is a tricky yet fruitful process, which demands a combination of numerical and verbal analytical processes. With the help of the strategic approach and high-tech tools that provide valuable insights into their content success rates, marketers will be able to transform their approaches to marketing to be more effective and more accurate.

Content Marketing Trends

Content marketing continuously changes depending on the technologies available and the reorganization of consumer preferences. Over the last few years, some of the essential trends have been developed, which have influenced the marketing ideas of marketers all over the world. The growth of personalized content is one of the major trends. Consumer experiences have now changed, and people expect personalized experiences that are connected to their personal needs and preferences. Data analytics and machine learning technologies have enabled this change by providing marketers with the ability to derive an understanding of consumer behavior and create the relevant content that resonates with their audience.

The other notable trend is the emergence of interactive content that is much more beneficial to users than conventional content. This features quizzes, polls, augmented reality experiments, and interactive videos. This type of content not only holds up attention but literally invites it to become actively involved, thus resulting in increased engagement and retention rates. With consumers growing familiar with interactivity, brands are beginning to factor this need into their content plans.

Visuals are keeping their leading position with video in the first place. Video is an essential element to content marketing, thanks to the fame of such sites as YouTube, TikTok, and Instagram. Short videos, in particular, have taken off, as they contain easy-to-consume interesting content, and can easily be incorporated into the high-paced browsing world. This trend gives marketers an opportunity to use genuine, relatable, and relational video content that connects with their target audiences.

Another trend shifting the content flow and creation toward a new reality is artificial intelligence implementation. These AI tools are also used to automate the creation of content, create better distribution strategies, and enhance the user experience. The technologies allow marketers to create great content en masse, which is both consistent and efficient across the channels.

There has also been an evolution of content marketing to more realistic and transparent communication. The more polished the brand messages are, the more consumers are wary of them and are opting, instead, to have genuine interactions. That is why the user-generated content and influencer collaboration are emerging: an ordinary person can give her/his experience and knowledge. This kind of authenticity leads to the element of trust and credibility, creating more intimate relationships between the brands and the audiences.

The items closely related to content marketing approaches include sustainability and social responsibility. Now, the brands must show their concern for environmental and social problems in their content. This is not only practicing these things but also ensuring that their business operations pass muster in terms of the values that they advocate. Brands that can be viewed as socially responsible promote more consumer involvement.

Moreover, one can hardly overestimate the relevance of omnichannel content strategies. Marketers are paying attention to the consistency and unity of messages that they use on various platforms to give a coherent brand experience. This will help because it does not matter which medium a consumer uses to interact, as they will get the same message through the brand.

This is a sign of how dynamic digital marketing in general has been, as the evolution of content marketing bears testament to this fact. Marketers can utilize these trends as a way of tapping into the needs of consumers currently and in the future, since they understand the changes taking place in the digital environment. To keep up with these changes and stay relevant, adaptability is the only success factor in the competitive world of content marketing.

It is ultimately important to learn all we can in AI, but we should put that knowledge to good use in solving actual issues. Educating themselves, connecting with others, and attending relevant events helps individuals and businesses keep up with AI developments and make use of new opportunities as they appear.

CHAPTER 5

SOCIAL MEDIA MARKETING

Platform Selection

When it comes to digital marketing, platform selection is one of the most decisive decisions the company can make, and it could largely affect the effectiveness of a marketing strategy. The realm of the digital world is broad and multifold, and it provides a variety of platforms, not all of which have the same particular qualities, which define the target market in demographic terms or the capability to engage. To choose the appropriate platform, one ought to be able to draw a thorough picture of the business goals, who the intended audience will be, and what kind of content will be released.

The initial stage of the platform selection is the target audience profile. Various platforms address diverse users with different behaviors. Considering the example of LinkedIn, professionals and companies mostly occupy the platform, and it is therefore a perfect choice when it comes to B2B marketing. In contrast, Instagram and TikTok can be considered the platforms of choice when it comes to reaching millennials and Gen Z audiences. This is why the audience is one of the major factors to be taken into account when determining the selection of platforms.

It is also critical to consider the platform that is aligned with the marketing objectives of the brand. When it comes to raising the level of brand awareness, Facebook and Instagram may be relevant social platforms since they have high user activity and share information. On the other hand, when the goal is to make a direct sale or conversion, Google Ads or Amazon may be more profitable, as each platform has an excellent advertising infrastructure and a shopping feature.

The type and format of the content are the other key aspects of choosing the platform. Instagram, Pinterest, and YouTube are social networks where visual content reigns as the means of communicating in the form of pictures and video clips. Conversely, Twitter and LinkedIn are more appropriate in terms of articles, thought leadership, and industry insights. Therefore, it is important to learn about the content strategy and how it is used in line with the platform's strengths.

The other considerations are the advertising capacity and tools of the platform. Some have advanced targeting features, analytics, and integration, which can be used to fuel marketing. Such options as the detailed audience targeting/retargeting on Facebook (and keyword targeting and much reach provided by Google Ads via search and display network) allow broadening the focus and tie the accounts to a particular topic or concept.

Budget issues also determine platform selection. Different sources might need more investment to reach and get a high engagement rate, whereas some might be cheaper. Replacing costs against possible gains from investment is a necessary step to ensure that marketing activities are considered cost-effective.

And finally, the competition cannot be left out. The study of area competition inhabitancy can also give clues on possible opportunities or existing gaps in the market. However, caution must be taken not to overemphasize this point and neglect innovation and differentiation so that the choice of the platform reflects unique brand positioning and does not resemble an industry fad.

To conclude, it is a complex process to choose the appropriate digital platform based on several criteria such as the audience profile, marketing task, the type of content, advertisement options, financial costs, or rivalry concerns. An efficient plan for selecting the platform can maximize the results of the digital marketing efforts, meaning getting the message of the brand to the right person at the right time, which will lead to business success.

Creating a Social Media Calendar

Designing a social media calendar is one of the critical moves towards the realization of a powerful D-marketing strategy. Its mechanism presupposes careful planning and strategic thinking, and each of the posts must be relevant to the entire business agenda and future objectives, and appealing to the target demographic. The calendar is like a roadmap, which shows marketers the way through the maze of content distribution on different platforms.

Designing a social media calendar in the first stage is impossible without an understanding of the goals of the brand and the likes of the viewer. The identification of key messages and themes can help marketers prepare content that is not only effective but entertaining and enlightening at the same time. This entails picking a variety of content forms, including blog posts, infographics, videos, and user-generated content, but all of them play a different role in the marketing funnel.

In the success of social media posts, timing is a very important aspect. A good calendar would also consider which time of day each platform should be posted, considering the traffic flow of the audience on each platform. This guarantees that content will be delivered to the audience at a place where they are most likely to be able to engage. The calendar also makes it possible to plan key dates and events, including product launch, holidays, and industry events, for every post to be more effective.

The basis of a stable and uniform presence in social media is organization. A well-organized calendar gives an accurate preview of the forthcoming content, and the marketers can identify the loopholes and possibilities of further interaction. The calendar can be efficiently created and managed with the help of such tools as spreadsheets, project management software, or even specialized social media management. The features provided by these tools, e.g., content scheduling, collaboration, and analytics, cannot be overestimated in terms of improving the social media strategy over time.

Another important factor of a social media calendar is flexibility. It is necessary to plan, but the propensity to fit in with the current events and trending topics may be a great way to increase engagement. Spontaneity by marketers must also be allowed so that content can be produced even when it takes advantage of current events or what goes viral. This versatility makes the brand very current and attentive to the volatile digital world.

Continuous self-improvement of a social media strategy comprises monitoring and analysis. The consistent review of the post performance will help marketers learn what the audience finds relevant and use this information to make further content decisions. Whether it is the engagement rate, reach, or conversions, these metrics ensure the success of the calendar and help to improve it.

Designing a social media calendar is not a process that is completed once, but it must be done regularly and meticulously. It is a very thin line between planning, creativity, and responsiveness in order to create a vigorous bond with the audience. Through careful planning and management of the calendar, marketers can make sure that their use of social media actually helps in achieving the goals of the brand in terms of marketing. Such orderly measures not only increase the visibility of the brand but also construct a dedicated following of active supporters, resulting in long-term success in the online world.

Engagement and Interaction

Amidst the continuously changing environment of online marketing, the issues of engagement and interaction have become two of the key components determining the effectiveness of a given online strategy. Since companies are interested in reaching out to their audiences, it is important to learn the intricacies of such factors. The engagement is a concept that involves the intensity of interest and involvement of the users in the content of a brand and the activities that a user engages in, including liking, commenting, sharing, and being on a site. Interaction, however, is a more active term when the brand actively communicates with the audience, usually through social media, chatbots, and customer service systems.

Upon achieving effective interaction with its target audience, the development of meaningful engagement demands insightful knowledge on the preferences and behaviors of the people being served. This is the aspect of creating content that will appeal to the demographic being targeted, using data analytics to provide an understanding of the interests of the users and catering the strategy according to the results of the analytics. Engagement is fostered with the help of quality and relevant content, which prompts the user not only to consume but also to engage in content that the brand provides. Images and videos are important visual material that attracts attention and catalyzes the action of users.

The next stage of the engagement continuum is interaction, when brands speak with their audience, actively engaging with the audience, building bonds and trust. This includes commenting, answering questions, and engaging in discussions that are relevant to the audience. The use of customized interactions, thanks to technologies like artificial intelligence and machine learning, allows brands to respond to each user, customizing the responses to make them feel connected and increasing customer satisfaction.

The use of social media as part of digital marketing has transformed how a brand talks and receives its audience. Social media applications such as Facebook, Instagram, Twitter, and LinkedIn present a good soil where the brands can interact simultaneously with users in real-time, enabling the brands to give or receive immediate feedback and response. In addition to making the reach of a brand massive, social media gives marketers a great insight into the sentiment and trends of consumers so that they can perfect their strategies and influence the customer experience.

Additionally, the emergence of mobile technology has continued to change the nature of engagement and interaction. As users access content mainly through smartphones, it becomes the obligation of the brands to optimize the content to deliver a smooth experience to the users. Mobile applications, push messages, and mobile-friendly content are some of the first things that a marketer should incorporate into their arsenal to ensure that the brand is always in touch with its audience.

Engagement and interaction as applied in the sphere of digital marketing are not just numbers but are carried out in order to establish long-term relationships with customers. The brands with the ability to develop authentic relationships with the audience tend to have a higher rate of loyalty and advocacy, and therefore higher brand equity and market share. With the ongoing digitalization of the world, the focus on engagement and interaction will continue to rise, thus pushing marketers to be creative and respond to the new demands of their audiences.

After all, the success of the strategy of engagement and interaction implies the capacity of the brand to listen, act, and adjust to the needs and wants of the audience. When emphasizing communicating authentically and paying attention to customer feedback, brands will be able to build a community of involved and loyal consumers who will be willing to go beyond simply becoming a consumer of the brand and become an advocate of its values and mission. It is also through the synergization between engagement and interaction as an element in this dynamic environment that sustains growth and success in digital marketing.

Analyzing Social Media Metrics

In an ever-changing digital marketing environment, social media metrics are the way to look into strategic approaches to gain awareness of the audience and their lifestyles. Social media provides an abundance of data points, when approached in an efficient manner, which can reveal information about the behavior of the consumers, the performance of specific content, and the overall health of the brand. As a compass in the sea, the interpretation of these values can be positioned as one of the guidelines that can help marketers make more educated choices in digital interactions.

The first thing that needs to be done when analyzing social media metrics is to know the key performance indicators (KPIs) that are also associated with the marketing objectives. Such KPIs differ depending on the platform and the objective, whether it is brand awareness, engagement, lead generation, or conversions. Typical metrics are likes, shares, comments, reach, impressions, and click-through rates. All of those metrics offer a narrower or wider perspective through which the success of social content can be reviewed.

The evidence of resonance and virality on content is likes and shares, as seen in the example. They depict what people think and feel in the moment and how much they are willing to promote the content by scattering it among their acquaintances. The comments, in their turn, provide more in-depth information on the audience interactions, though they involve some effort, unlike a mere click. The interpretation of the tone and content of the comments can reveal what people feel about it and what could be improved.

The terms reach and impressions can be easily interchanged, but they can provide different insights. Reach is counted as the value of the unique people who have been shown the content, and impressions are counted as the total number of times the content was shown, and this can be more than the numbers since a user might have seen the content several times. Learning about the metrics will assist marketers in their evaluation of the potential exposure of their content, along with what is actually displayed.

The use of click-through rates (CTR) plays an imperative role in determining the effectiveness of the call-to-action content on blogs. When CTR is high, it indicates that such content was strong enough to encourage the audience to take action as required, whether it is to visit a web page or subscribe to a newsletter, among others. On the other hand, a poor CTR could mean that the call-to-action has to be improved or that the target audience should be modified.

In addition to the simpler statistics, a more in-depth analysis is possible, i.e., observing engagement possibilities in relation to time to find out the trends and patterns. Such time analysis may allow understanding when content should be published to aim at the largest reach and interest. It can also assist in learning the lifecycle of a post and what makes it last longer or its viewer interest diminish.

The measures of social media are also of great importance in competitor analysis. The comparisons and contrasts of the industry standards and competitors will help an organization to see the gaps in its strategy and possibilities to differentiate itself. This comparative analysis can be used as a strategic change and as a motivational agent of innovation in content development.

A sentiment analysis in the metric of social media adds qualitative value to the quantitative measures. The tone and the feeling the user made the content in can be evaluated to allow the marketers to know the reputation of the brand and the emotional appeal of the campaign. It is the type of information that is most perfect to refine messages and make sure that they meet the expectations of a certain audience.

After all, that is the strength of the metrics of social media since it translates the raw data into insights that can be applied. Being agile with these metrics not only allows for overseeing the effectiveness of their work but also provides marketers with the ability to implement future actions with high accuracy and boldness. The tools are of the essence, and as the digital environment keeps improving, so should the manner in which we explore and apply them.

CHAPTER 6

EMAIL MARKETING STRATEGIES

Building an Email List

A key pillar in digital marketing is the development of an email list, which can be considered one of the crucial aspects of ensuring the effectiveness of a campaign. It can be compared to the development of a vibrant community, and every subscriber is a person and a networking member who can be an enthusiast of the brand.

The target audience should be identified as the first step in this complex process. It is important to learn who the prospective subscribers are, along with what they value and how they will communicate with digital content. The same is the rudder to the development of contents that hook them so that when the message is conveyed, it finds relevance and communication.

After the audience is identified, the second step will be creating interesting incentives that will make the visitors want to subscribe. These incentives may be in the form of what people call lead magnets. Whether it is royalty content in the form of ebooks or whitepapers, VIP access to features, or even discounts on products, they should be viewed as desirable by the audience. The trick here is to do it in such a way that will satisfy the interests and needs of the prospective subscribers and give them a tangible reason to sign up to receive emails.

The technical side of the email list construction is the establishment of an effective sign-up procedure. These involve creating forms in an easy-to-use manner, and they are readily available whether on the site or in the landing pages. These types must have very little information required so as to minimize friction and have more people registering. Another thing is to make sure these forms are mobile-friendly, as the number of people who consume the content on a mobile-based device is rising.

To further boost the list-building approach, one can make use of integration with social media platforms. Through the marketing of the email list on social platforms, the brands are in a position to utilize the available networks to reach a wider audience. It is not just a visibility tool, but also carries the advantage of the power of social proof, as the potential subscribers are exposed to the activity of other people interacting with the brand.

The other important element is list hygiene. Cleaning the list can be done frequently by removing those subscribers who are not responding to the list, which keeps the list active and attentive. The same facilitates a high sender reputation, which is something very important to make sure that the emails reach the inbox and not the spam box.

The performance of the email list is continually analyzed. Marketers can keep track of activities like the open rate, click-through rate, and conversion rates in order to gauge what is and is not succeeding. One may optimize the content and the strategy based on this intelligence, which will guarantee that the email list remains an excellent resource that is part of the marketing toolkit.

Finally, an e-mail list is not always about collecting emails; it is about developing a medium through which people are able to have a meaningful interaction with one another. It needs a tactical approach, and this is where creativity meets technical expertise and thorough knowledge about the audience. With attentive cultivation and continual improvement, an email list may transform into one of the most effective tools the digital marketer has in terms of growing the company and maintaining a long-term relationship with customers.

Crafting Effective Emails

Emails are one of the strongest tools that can be used in the digital marketing industry. The secret to creating great emails is to place themselves in the position of the target audience, provide value, and adhere to the tone that the reader might find appealing. Email messages must start by having the recipient ignore an effective subject line, which will motivate them to read the message.

The first point of contact is the subject line. It is essential to make it interesting, but not too informative, so as to help give a preview of what it is about. This can be a very effective strategy in making an email alluring because the recipient will feel respected and to the point of knowing him or her. It is possible to use the name of the recipient or base the presentation on past interactions to present the impression of familiarity and relatedness.

After opening the email, the relevance must be achieved as quickly as possible in the introductory part. A recipient should have his or her needs or interests directly appealed to, and the purpose of the email must also correlate with the expectations of the recipient. Clearness and brevity are important in this case since the introduction of too much detail may prove to be a put-off. Bullet points or short paragraphs can be used to put across the message effectively.

The message of the email must follow up on the promises created by the subject and the introduction. It must contain rich information-valuable information, it may contain offers and news. The interest of the reader can be retained by the formulation of the content into a logical flow of patterns. Choices that increase engagement can also include the use of visual content, i.e., images or infographics, to divide the text into pieces and explain important information. Nonetheless, one needs to make sure that these aspects can be viewed properly when the email is opened to prevent hindrance to the display.

Effective emails cannot be complete without call-to-action (CTA) statements. They lead the recipient through to where one wants them to be, whether on a page that allows him or her to download something, visit a website, or buy something. CTAs need to be direct, strong, and placed well in the message. Action declarative words may persuade the reader to act to the next step.

The email tone and the style must portray the voice of the brand in a certain way, and the preferences of the audience must be kept in mind. Such a friendly professional tone can be effective, as it is not too casual, but not too formal as well. Brand uniformity in terms of style will strengthen the brand and enable it to develop confidence with people.

There is also timing and frequency, which play a part in the effectiveness of emails. Timing can dramatically improve both open and click-through rates, and can therefore be considered an important aspect. Another thing that has to be avoided is the excess mailing of too many emails to the people, so that they end up unsubscribing or marking the email address as spam.

Lastly, it is important to test and analyze email performance to ascertain its continued performance. Testing such aspects as subject lines or CTAs with A/B approaches can deliver some indication of what can best appeal to the reading users. Selecting the monitoring parameters, such as the open rate, the click-through rate, and the conversion, also aids in optimization and successful further development of the email campaigns.

The development of successful emails comes as the result of a tactical, yet creative approach to email. Emails can be an effective part of any digital marketing strategy, and it is possible to achieve this by paying attention to the value delivery and the need to retain the audience.

Automation and Segmentation

Automation and segmentation are the two game-changers of an ever-changing world of digital marketing. These aspects transform the way business communicates with the audience and simplify their operations to enhance efficiency and effectiveness.

Digital marketing automation is the technique that utilizes technology to automate a number of routine tasks that require no human input. This saves time and is accurate and consistent in various channels. Automation helps marketers to post on social media, give personalised emails, and manage advertising campaigns that require less manual analysis. Its advantages are numerous: they involve productivity, better lead nurturing, and customer experiences. The aspects of automation software are that they can examine the habits and system of the user, and the system permits the marketer to introduce the content and offers that would be of value to the individual customer.

Segmentation, in its turn, refers to breaking down an extensive audience into smaller and more approachable groups according to a particular parameter like demographics, behavior, or interest. This strategy will help marketers to send their messages more accurately, and thus it is more likely to be involved and converted. The segmentation enables the design of very customized marketing processes that take into consideration the different needs and preferences of the respective groups. The nature of each segment is very different, and by knowing the unique nature of each of these segments, businesses can make each of them come face to face with information that is relevant to their interest and needs.

The synergy between automation and segmentation is the real strength of digital marketing. When these are coupled, the marketers shall be in a position to pass the correct message to the correct person at the correct time. Automation will be useful in conveying these messages effectively, whereas segmentation will make these messages meaningful and effective. As an example, an automated email campaign can be divided to address various customer segments with offers specific to them, which leads to increased open and conversion rates.

More than that, automation and segmentation help provide useful insights into consumer behavior. Marketers are able to see patterns and trends in the data collected in automated campaigns and use them in subsequent strategies. Segmentation also narrows down this information further and gives an in-depth view as to what motivates various consumer segments. This is a data-driven strategy that gives businesses the ability to respond to changes within consumer preferences and market conditions in real-time.

Nonetheless, automation and segmentation are functions that need to be ready and carried out within the department. Marketers have to make sure that the technology they employ is not inconsistent with their general approach and goal. One needs to choose the best tools that will provide the flexibility and scalability required to scale up the business. Also, the marketers will always have to keep an eye on their campaign, making adjustments and regular updates to be sure that they are running the campaign the way they want it, on target.

It is not a habit but a requirement that business entities would integrate automation and segmentation in their digital marketing procedures to remain competitive in the digital-first world. The future of marketing will merely grow and develop with these strategies as a way of improving it, because a strong success rate will soon be achieved with them. With the right use of automation and segmentation, businesses will establish deeper connections with their audiences and engage them, thus accomplishing their marketing objectives.

Measuring Email Campaigns

At the juncture of the complex world of digital marketing, the need to assess the success of email campaigns could hardly be overestimated. It is essential to know what metrics determine success in email marketing to address the approach by decreasing or increasing engagement. Analyzing and measuring these parts enables marketers to gain more out of their campaigns.

Measurement of email campaigns starts by recognizing key performance indicators (KPI) that are in line with the purpose of the campaign. Such KPIs normally incorporate open rates, click-through rates (CTR), conversion rates, bounce rates, and unsubscribe rates. All these measurements give an idea about the various parts of campaign success. As an example, the open rate shows how well the subject line was and the email send timing, and the click-through rate shows how engaging the email content is.

Open rates act as a first measurement of success. They capture the degree to which the subject line is appealing to the audience as well as the suitability of the time the email goes to the recipient in relation to his/her schedule. Having a higher open rate is an indication that the subject line was interesting enough to make the recipients open the email.

Click-through rates, in turn, explore the interaction of the recipient with the content of the email more thoroughly. This measurement shows how well the design of the email was and whether the call-to-action (CTA) was clear. A great CTR means that the message was interesting and the CTA pitch was effective in making the recipient desire to act further.

Another important measure is conversion rate or the percentage of people who did what you wanted them to do, i.e., buy a product or subscribe to a newsletter. It is commonly estimated that such a measure is the final yardstick of an email campaign achieved since it is directly proportional to revenue and business growth.

It is mandatory to watch the bounce rates as a way of ensuring a healthy email list. An excessive amount of bounces may imply the problem of poor email deliverability, which outdated or wrongful email addresses could cause. This indicator assists marketers in having an uncluttered and effective email list, ensuring that they will be able to send messages to the intended audience.

The unsubscribe rates help to have visibility of the satisfaction of the users of the content fed and the emails sent. An increasing unsubscribe rate can indicate that something is wrong with the content or that the emails are being sent too often.

These primitive measurements can be supplemented with the use of advanced analytics to give more information. Heat maps can relate to an example in which they can be used to determine what portion of an email is being noticed by the user, and can assist marketers in knowing how users behave. A/B testing makes it possible to compare various items, including subject lines or CTAs, to find out which one is more productive.

Conversion of these metrics into a holistic analytics platform can help marketers make wise decisions. Through the constant re-analysis and alteration of strategies using such insights, marketers are capable of boosting the success of their email campaigns, thus ensuring better engagement and conversion rates. Email marketing is a very valuable means to achieve business success in the digital era, but it requires careful measurement and analysis to succeed.

CHAPTER 7

PAY-PER-CLICK ADVERTISING

Understanding PPC Models

Pay-per-click (PPC) models are one of the essential parts of digital marketing strategies since they provide a straightforward and measurable approach to digital businesses, reaching potential customers. In essence, PPC advertising is a web-based model in which the advertisers are charged a fee whenever their advertisement is clicked. The application is mainly employed to generate traffic to the sites with the intention of transforming the visitors into consumers, hence making sales or leads.

PPC models also work under a bidding mechanism, under which advertisers bid to have their advertisements placed on a search engine's sponsored links when someone does a keyword search that matches their business product or service. Such advertisements are visible on search engine results pages (SERP), therefore being very visible to users who are already interested in finding information or making purchases. The location of these advertisements depends on a factor that comprises the price that is bid and the quality, which is a measure of the relevancy of these types of ads relative to search words.

The quality score plays a very significant role in the PPC campaign since it determines the cost-per-click (CPC) and ad position. The quality score will present the opportunity of reduced costs and even good ad positions. Thus, advertisers should focus more on it as it can bring improved return on investment. The list of factors influencing the quality score is as follows: click-through rate (CTR); relevance of each keyword with its ad group, the landing page quality, and the ad text overall relevance.

PPC platforms exist in many forms, the most common one being Google Ads because they cover a sky-high audience and provide an exquisite number of targeting opportunities. There are other popular platforms, such as Bing Ads and social media outlets, like Facebook and Instagram, where PPC advertising can be bought with somewhat different dynamics and different opportunities to target the audiences.

The various forms of PPC ads should be known so that effective campaigns can be created. The most common one is search ads, which are shown on search engines and target specific questions using keywords. Instead, display advertisements are placed on web pages in the Google Display Network, and they are based on user preferences and web search activity instead of focused search terms.

Another strong point of PPC advertising is the ability to remarket, which enables a business to focus on users who did not convert despite visiting their site or using their application. This plan assists in re-engaging prospective customers by displaying suitable advertisements on various websites that they view.

PPC should be properly planned and executed. It commences by conducting heavy research on keywords to know the most relevant and cost-effective keywords to bid. It is also vital to develop interesting ad copy that can engage the target audience, thus directly influencing the CTR and quality score of the ad.

Ongoing monitoring and improvement are important in ensuring the success of PPC campaigns. This includes performance analysis, which includes determining the trend and making appropriate changes to the bids, keywords, and ad placements. A/B testing will also be useful in improving the decisions made during the campaign, since you will have a clear understanding of the aspects of the ads that are appealing to the audience.

In turn, PPC models are a dynamic and flexible form of digital advertising, allowing companies the means to reach their targeted clientele as effectively as possible. Learning and using the complexities of PPC is a way through which marketers can generate the desired traffic, enhance visibility of their brands, and fulfill their business goals in a better manner.

Creating Effective Ads

Before things can be made to work, it is an art that demands the ability to be creative, have a strategic approach, and understand the psychology of the consumer. Any successful ad campaign is derived from the fact that the ad catches attention and will carry a message or say something that is very appealing and relates well to the targeted people. Nowadays, when all consumers see numerous ads every day, it necessitates more than a catchy slogan and/or an attractive design to make a difference.

Before one creates a good advertisement, one would have to know his/her audience. The audience to whom the ad is being communicated is useful in framing the message to the precise requirements, inclinations, and behaviours of such a group. This includes carrying out an intense market research to come up with information concerning consumer behavior, tastes, and pain areas. This piece of information helps marketers produce advertisements that go beyond getting the attention of the readers or viewers to making an emotional appeal to the audience.

When the audience has been well established, the next step is to come up with a clear and concise message. The message must be straightforward, but effective in conveying what the product or service is all about. It must take care of the wants or needs of the audience and outline the advantages of using the brand over other brands. Less is more, because a confusing or overloaded message may easily lose the interest of the audience.

Visual aspects are important to the efficiency of an advertisement. Imagery, layout, color, and typography can play a significant role in the perception of an ad. The visuals ought to match the brand message and the same brand. They are supposed to supplement, but not to take over the message. A good advertisement contains visuals that the viewer can use their eye to follow and highlight the most important aspects of the message.

Alongside the visual, the tone and the style of the advertisement are important aspects since they are used to elicit an emotional response from the audience. Regardless of whether the advert is of a comic, motivating, or educational nature, the voice used must reflect the nature of the brand and appeal to the intended audience. Uniformity in tone among various platforms and the form of the advertisements contributes to the development of brand recognition and credibility.

In addition, ad placement and time are some of the important factors of an ad strategy. Knowing the location and time of day the target market is most likely to see an advertisement can play a great role in making the ad effective. This includes using the appropriate platforms, be it social media, search engines, or conventional media, and placing the ad at a place and time when the activity of the media is at its peak.

Last, but not least, the testing and optimization should be done to guarantee the continuous success of an ad campaign. The marketers can determine what is effective and what is not by examining some of the key performance indicators used (such as click-through rates, conversion rates, and the level of engagement). This fact-based procedure enables the constant optimization and change of the advertising plan to achieve the most impressive effects and the highest rate of occurrence.

Effective ads are designed in a dynamic process, and to come up with such ads, one must understand the audience and the digital environment well. The idea of adopting an innovative approach to storytelling in business while integrating the aspect of strategic planning and data analysis enables marketers to create an advertisement that not only attracts attention but also provides a useful outcome.

Budgeting for PPC

The ability to create a balanced Pay-Per-Click (PPC) advertising budget is among the first things that one should think about when formulating a digital marketing strategy. Although PPC advertising is a very effective tool that enables companies to reach their target audience by targeting them specifically, this will only work when proper planning and resources are allocated towards the execution aspect. Once you know how PPC budgeting can be complex, the difference between a successful campaign and a lost spending can be determined.

The essence of the PPC budgeting is to figure out how to finance marketing objectives. It starts by having a clear definition of what the business intends to do with its PPC campaigns. Depending on the aim of the increased brand awareness, buying traffic or website visitors, leads generation, and sales promotion, the allocated funding should be allocated. Setting these objectives gives a platform on which a budget may be set and changes may be made accordingly.

The second stage is to conduct a detailed analysis of the competitive environment. Becoming conversant with the market realities, such as the cost-per-click (CPC) within the market, assists in making reasonable budget expectations. Such tools as Google Ads Keyword Planner may provide some experience in the specifics of bidding, and help businesses know how much it can cost to target a certain keyword. This type of information is essential for establishing a subsistence budget that guarantees competitiveness without incurring many expenses.

A major element in PPC budgeting is how much one spends on various campaigns as well as ad groups. Spreading out is essential in reducing the risk and maximizing coverage. Investing in several campaigns enables any business to conveniently experiment with various strategies and determine those that can yield a higher level of investment. It is also flexible with this method, and the marketer can move money to the more successful campaigns as the information becomes known.

Analysis and continuous monitoring are a part and parcel of PPC budgeting. Checking the rate metrics on the campaign performance, i.e., click through (CTR), conversion rate, and cost per acquisition (CPA) on a regular basis, provides adequate insights to make the necessary budget changes. This is a data-driven technique that will make sure that the budget is being utilized efficiently and that it can inform of areas that require the budget to be either boosted or cut.

Moreover, businesses need to be ready for various fluctuations during the year and changes in the market that may affect PPC performance. Having some reserves of the budget enables us to make immediate changes when something new is available or arises. Such flexibility is essential in ensuring that campaign initiatives are maintained and that trends or competitive advantages are taken advantage of.

Automation and artificial intelligence tools are the other factors to consider when budgeting for PPC. The technologies are able to improve bidding strategies in real-time, thus operating with maximum efficiency of the budget available. The usage of automated bidding allows one to make adjustments to bids, depending on different factors, such as time, device, and location of the user, which can substantially improve the work of the campaign without spending much money.

Last, the PPC budget should be revisited frequently and updated as an ongoing element of the digital marketing strategy. The resource allocation should change with the changing market conditions and business objectives of an organization. Frequent budget reviews and adjustments help make sure that there is also alignment between PPC work and the general marketing goals, and that it keeps providing value.

Essentially, budgeting PPC is not an activity, but a process that should be planned accordingly, observed, and adjusted systematically. PPC advertising can greatly assist businesses in meeting their marketing objectives by comparing the critical factors involved and being ready to make changes.

Analyzing PPC Performance

Pay-per-click (PPC) marketing is one of the central aspects of digital marketing in the sense that businesses can become more visible and reach customers with online advertising services after targeting the potential audience. PCC campaigns cannot be left without thinking of how to evaluate their performance because this will ensure the returns on such investments are what is expected. It has several aspects and criteria that should be analyzed carefully so that the overall picture of the performance of these campaigns can be revealed with references to the areas that should be changed.

To begin with, it is necessary to learn the important metrics. A click-through rate (CTR) is one of the main measurements of the effectiveness of an ad and its appeal to the viewers. A large CTR implies that the viewers liked the ad content and targeting, whereas a low CTR implies adjustment in either the messages or the targeting of the viewer. Another important indicator would be conversion rate, which shows what proportion of the clicks lead to a wanted action, showing how many people out of clicks may make a purchase or sign up, etc. This metric shows the efficiency of the landing page as well as the user experience after the first touch of this advertisement.

Financial Cost-per-click(CPC) and cost-per-acquisition (CPA) are financial measures of the cost-efficiency of a PPC campaign. CPC denotes what is being expended per click, whereas CPA depicts the cost of obtaining a client. It is desirable to monitor these metrics to gain insight into the cost of PPC activity and optimize the budget.

Ideally, it is meant to minimize these expenditures whilst keeping or expanding the conversion rate.

In addition, it is essential to analyze the quality of the ads. Quality score is a convenience employed by search engines in evaluating the relevance and quality of keywords, ads, and landing pages. Within the PPC strategy, the high-quality score will result in a decrease in CPCs and improved ad placements, hence its importance. Refining ad relevance, landing page experience, and keyword selection are some of the activities that can be conducted to improve quality scores.

The other point of consideration will be the role of ad extensions. Other snippets in the form of site links, callouts, etc., may be used to add additional information to an AD and offer new causes to click. The tests on the performance of these extensions may provide some answers about what information the users consider useful and how it can influence the overall ad performance.

PPC performance can also be analyzed by data segmentation, contributing to the identification of trends and patterns. This segmentation can be done through factors such as the type of devices, geographic segments, demographics, and hours. This kind of detailed analysis can help determine which parts are doing well and which ones need fixing. For example, if the rate of conversion is higher among mobile users, investing more in mobile-based advertisements can pay off.

Lastly, A/B testing is one of the pillars of measuring performance. Marketers can also test the various ad variations to identify which aspects have the greatest impact on success. This may include testing various headlines, action text, or images. One can make better decisions and campaigns based on the ideas obtained through A/B testing, which makes the campaigns more effective.

This boils down to the fact that a glistening approach to PPC performance analysis can take a digital marketing strategy a long way. Concentrating on these important indications, financial effectiveness, quality scores, ad extensions, distinguishing data, around-the-clock testing, the companies are able to streamline their PPC products to get a higher perceptibility, interest, and eventually, conversion.

CHAPTER 8

INFLUENCER MARKETING

Identifying the Right Influencers

There is a large ecosystem of digital marketing, and defining the appropriate influencers is the key to a successful strategy. This process starts by having a clear insight into what the brand stands for and what message it is to create. Knowledge is important, as it provides the basis for how influencers should be chosen, and as long as their brand fits the company, these people will be genuine and consistent in their messages.

A careful analysis of the followers of the influencer should follow the second phase. It is not only the number of the following but the quality of relevance and involvement of that following. A lower but more engaged audience profile may be much more valuable than a higher but less engaged audience, which does not align as closely with the target demographic of the brand. This involves examining the measures like demographics of the intended audiences, engagement of the intended audiences, and the kinds of content that such audiences are most responsive to.

Furthermore, it is critical to look into the style and voice of the influencer. The influencer must include the products or services of the brand in their content in a natural way so that it will not be unusual and artificial, but will be connected organically. It seeks people who are already doing this, who have been known to develop material that can support what the brand seeks to say, and in a manner that is genuine and right.

The last important thing is the degree of skills and authority of the influencer in his/her field. An influencer is also perceived as an expert or thought leader in their industry, and therefore, they can give credibility to a brand, which improves its perception and consumer trust. Thus, the brands must identify influencers with a history of success as experts and deliver the message of the brand through the frames of their authority.

Moreover, the previous projects and the influencer should be evaluated. This involves the assessment of the success of the past campaigns in which they have been involved and how they have interacted with brands in the past. One should also ask a question about how well those collaborations ran and whether the influencer was professional and reliable enough to carry through with it.

Another method of the selection process is knowing the influencer's values and their compatibility with the brand. In the modern, socially motivated market, consumers are more concerned about supporting the brands that match their beliefs and value systems. Consequently, the opinion of an influencer sharing the same values will fill in the gap between the brand and its consumers, making the relationship even more trustworthy and loyal.

Lastly, the option of a long-term partnership must be embraced. The process of establishing a long-term relationship with an influencer may be more helpful than a single campaign since it helps to establish a stronger connection with his or her audience. This involves evaluating how eager the influencer is to be in a long-lasting relationship and how he or she can develop to suit the requirements of the brand.

By attentively approaching these factors, brands will be well placed to align and partner strategically with the right influencers, thus enabling their digital marketing campaigns to reach an advanced height where they come into contact with the target demographic. This strategic practice not only widens the dissemination of the brand but also guarantees the dissemination of the brand message with sincerity and influence.

Building Relationships

Within the vast scenery of digital marketing, the nature of relationship-building establishment stands out as a success factor. It is essential to develop meaningful and long-lasting relationships at the core of this process that go beyond the conventional scope of transactional relations. With the digital world filling up with content and options, it is increasingly likely that merely existing as a brand is not nearly enough to make a meaningful connection with the audience.

Building relationships in digital marketing is based on knowing the audience well. It starts with a thorough search to determine the demands, tastes, and patterns of the potential population. This appreciation enables the marketers to ensure that their strategies will appeal to the audience in a personal way. With personal data analytics tools and survey responses, marketers can know what pains and drives their users to be able to develop messages that directly address the customer on a specific level.

Authenticity also has an instrumental role in establishing trust and loyalty. In this era, consumers are bombarded with advertisement messages, and authenticity pierces through them. The most effective brands are those that speak out openly and frequently and remain faithful to themselves, which makes them more trustworthy in the mind of the audience. What must be done here is not only to make the messages honest but also to make the actions of the brand match the values and expressions of the brand. People form a long-term bond with a brand when they find it authentic and thus get inclined to interact with it.

Another significant part of relationship-building is engagement, which can be proactive and reactive. Proactive engagement is the practice of contacting audiences with the help of multiple sources, including social media, email marketing, and content. The interactions must be geared toward adding value, whether this be in the form of great information, enjoyable tales, or troubleshooting. Reactive engagement, in turn, consists of answering questions, responding to complaints from the audience, and resolving issues as quickly and successfully as possible. This is a two-way communication that creates a feeling of belonging and communicates to audiences that they are listened to and appreciated.

Personalization also maximizes the interrelationship between the brands and their audiences. Using technology, marketers should be able to provide an individualized experience that will be based on the personal interests and preferences of the individual. This may include individualized email marketing as well as specific product suggestions. By sending content and offers to customers that are relevant to them, the people end up feeling understood and liked, and their attachment to the brand increases.

In addition, community building adds to the aspect of developing relationships in digital marketing on an individual level. Performing on the stage and setting up places where people can communicate with each other, share experiences, and support others, establishes the climate of belonging. This is possible via forums on the internet, social media circles, or even events hosted by the brand. Besides increasing brand loyalty, such communities become a rich source of feedback and innovation.

In the end, relationship development in digital marketing is a continuous practice that needs time and flexibility. Relationship-building strategies require evolution as technological and consumer behaviour changes. Focusing on comprehending, authenticity, immersion, customization, and societal connection, the brands will be able to connect with their consumers in a meaningful but also durable way, opening the door to long-term profitability in the online market.

Measuring Influencer Impact

In the ever-changing environment of online marketing, influencers have come to play a central role, where they mold the perception of consumers and generate potential buyers. Measuring the extent of their influence, however, raises a multifaceted problem for marketers who want to justify the investments and maximize strategies. To know the impact of such digital avatars, a complex approach has to be taken, comprising a range of measurements and methods of analysis.

At the heart of gauging the influence of the influencer lies the examination of the engagement metrics. Such metrics give information on the behaviors of audiences who consume the information posted by influencers. Such elements as likes, shares, comments, and the general outreach of posts by an influencer should be key metrics. All these metrics provide a glimpse of the degree of interest and activity on the part of the audience. Nonetheless, it is essential to pay attention to the numbers only to find further explanations, taking into consideration the mood behind the comments and the context in which things are shared.

The other key element is the test of conversion rates. This is the monitoring of the route that the consumer goes through after exposure to the influencer material until a specific identity or operation, like purchase or signing up to receive a newsletter, has been accomplished. Conversion rates/rate are an effective measure of the capacity of an influencer to elicit real outcomes on behalf of a brand. Through the use of tools such as unique tracking links and discount codes, it is possible to attribute sales and other conversions to the individual influencers, which gives a better indication of the individual influencer.

The concepts of brand awareness and perceptions are also significant factors during the evaluation of the effectiveness of influencers. The Influencers tend to become brand ambassadors, and when they are connected to a brand, it can cause a huge transformation in the perception of the population. Pre-and Post-Surveys and brand sentiment analysis may be conducted to measure consumer attitudes towards influencer campaigns. Such qualitative information will complement quantitative measures, which will provide an overview of the activity of an influencer.

Besides these metrics, there is also an important metric of how much a particular investment will yield, which is referred to as the return on investment (ROI) of the influencer partnerships. How to calculate ROI is the question of the difference between the amount it takes to involve an influencer and the financial rewards of the collaboration. Such a study will assist in measuring whether the influencer effect is worth the cost. High-fidelity analysis tools and models may help to correlate the activities of the influencers with changing revenues and help marketers make decisions based on data.

Other factors that affect the measurement of impacts are the selection of the influencers. Influencers are not equal; they can be effective or rather ineffective depending on the demographics of their audience, level of engagement, and niche they are specialized in. Thus, the most important thing is to choose the correct influencers who must match the brand values and audiences. And the statistics of an overlap in the audience and engagement rates may help to find the most suitable influencers to use in a campaign.

In addition, one cannot neglect the long-term impact of influencer marketing. Although immediate measures can give an overview of the success of the campaign, the brand loyalty effect and customer retention can even be more useful. These secondary effects can be detected only through longitudinal studies and continuous observation of how the customer is engaged, and they provide answers to questions regarding how customer engagement will remain a long-term effect of digital marketing undertakings.

In such a fluid digital world, determining the influence of an influencer is an art and a science. A combination of quantitative and qualitative data helps marketers grasp the multidimensional influencer effect on consumer behavior and the success of a business. Such a holistic picture is beneficial not only in influencing the power of campaigns with the help of influencers but also in reinforcing the entire digital marketing plan.

Trends in Influencer Marketing

Over the last few years, influencer marketing has turned into a major part of digital marketing campaigns, shifting out of niche strategy. Since brands always aspire to create genuine relationships with their audiences, engaging with the range and interest of influencers is increasingly becoming more critical. Influencer marketing has a series of emerging trends that are changing the face of influencer marketing.

Among the most considerable trends, it is possible to note the transfer to micro and nano influencers. They are not as big as the traditional celebrities or mega influencers, but they have more dedicated followers. Companies realize the market potential of reaching out to such influencers, as recommendations from these people are usually received more sincerely and credibly by their audience. Such change is motivated by the need for authenticity and the realization that smaller influencers can provide more specific and efficient interaction.

Increasingly, video content is becoming more important, too. TikTok and Instagram Reels platforms have become the most popular, and they push influencers to make exciting video content and engage the audience. The format is not only more creative but also fits consumer needs of fast and interesting media. Consequently, brands are partnering with such influencers who are excellent at creating video content so as to boost their promotional approach.

There is also the trend of influencer marketing, which is also being driven by the development of social commerce. Social media platforms have become more shopper-friendly, and users can now buy products and stories that are posted on them. Influencers have a key role to play in such an ecosystem, as the role they play is to help followers in the buying process by either giving them exclusive discounts or insights about products. This smooth introduction of commerce to social media interactions further points to influencer marketing being an even better tool in generating sales.

In addition, long-term partnerships between brands and influencers are becoming a major focus. Brands no longer want one-off partnerships with influencers, instead preferring long-term relationships in which they can familiarise those who influence with their product or services and use them as a real advocate of their company. The trend is associated with greater insight into the role played by influencers in defining the brand perception and inspiring continual consumer loyalty.

The emergence of new platforms and technologies also determines the strategy of influencer marketing. As virtual influencers and augmented reality enter the business world, brands are trying new methods of action to appeal to consumers. Although virtual influencers are not ordinary individuals, they can be highly tailored and provide brands with new options for storytelling. Similarly, influencer campaigns could also be enriched through augmented reality experiences, which offer interactive and immersive content to ensure that audiences are kept fascinated.

Influencer marketing is also becoming increasingly data-driven in its decision-making. Through analytics, brands are looking into the KPIs of allvisor campaigns they are using, including the levels of engagement, conversions, and ROI. This analytical method will help marketers improve their strategies, identify influencers, promote their brand, and reach the target audience.

Lastly, ethics are becoming increasingly important in influencer marketing. The primary importance of transparency and authenticity lies in the fact that people get to know more about the mechanisms of advertising as consumers. There is also a growing responsibility among influencers and brands to label their partnerships and for them to represent sponsored content. This change of heart in ethical marketing is crucial in winning consumer confidence and having meaningful relationships.

In general, most of the tendencies in influencer marketing center towards an active and developing division. As brands keep finding their way in this terrain, they have to stay flexible and dynamic and adopt new channels and approaches that will ensure that they can reach out and tap the target audiences. The potential of influencer marketing is the possibility of evolving as consumer behaviors and technology have changed and are going to change. It, therefore, remains a very crucial element of a digital marketing strategy.

CHAPTER 9

AFFILIATE MARKETING

Setting Up an Affiliate Program

When developing an affiliate program in the complex tapestry of digital marketing, it is possible to compare the design of such a program to the stage preparation of a dramatic event. The first ones are essential as they must have a proper understanding of the goals and objectives that are meant to be attained by the program. It should start with finding the target audience and the niche in which the affiliate program is going to operate. It includes attractively studying the market trends, consumer behavior, and competitor strategies in order to secure a niche in the digital market.

After the basics are settled, a potential affiliate needs a value proposition that is attractive enough. This will be in terms of developing appealing commission structures, bonuses, and rewards, which will suit the financial objectives of the business, e.g., targets, as well as the interests of the affiliates. The terms and conditions of the program have to be transparent to make clear to the affiliates that they are reasonably informed of what is expected of them and what they stand to gain out of it.

Another important factor is the choice of the appropriate affiliate management platform. This is the core of the program, which will help with easy operations and business interactions between the affiliates and the business. Ease of use, capacity to integrate with the systems already in use, and deployment of strong reporting and tracking tools should also be considered well so as to satisfy the program's needs.

Affiliate Recruitment is a tactical procedure that needs a multifaceted approach. Potential affiliates can also be attracted by using the available networks, extending contacts via social media, attending industry forums, etc. It is also good to develop an interesting pitch where the special selling points of the program and the advantages of the partnership can be seen.

The work of training and helping supporters of affiliates is the most important part of the program. By offering all available learning materials like webinars, tutorials, and instructional guides, the affiliates will be better equipped with the knowledge and tools necessary to market the products or services. Periodic contact with the affiliates is accomplished with newsletters and updates, which will help them remain connected and aware of the new trends, promotions, and opportunities in the program.

Watching the performance of the affiliate program and its improvement is a permanent process. Analytics and feedback mechanisms can be used to determine/determine what needs improvement and use data to make decisions on how to improve the effectiveness of the program. They might need to change the commission structures and marketing campaigns, as well as the support channels, to suit the new market dynamics and the feedback received from affiliates.

Creating the feeling of community among affiliates also makes the program much more successful. Inspiration and group dynamics can be built by establishing forums or social media groups where the affiliates have a chance to share their insights, experiences, and tips. Motivation might also be implemented through awarding or other valued incentives to the performing affiliates that will improve morale and the level of performance.

Essentially, establishing an affiliate program is a laborious procedure that is developed through thorough planning, implementation, and perfecting. With a firm ground base and managed affiliates, firms can gradually cover more ground and develop a more effective marketing campaign, which in the long run will lead to success and growth in the online world.

Choosing Affiliates

Choosing the best affiliates is a critical move in designing a winning digital marketing solution. It entails a close analysis of the possible sponsors that can market your brand really well and lead to sales. This is then followed by the identification of affiliates whose audience fits the bill of your target market. With this alignment, you deliver your marketing messages to the right people, thereby doubling the chances of them engaging with your messages and getting converted.

One of the key things when it comes to selecting affiliates is their level of influence and coverage in your targeted demographic. A large following of the affiliate networks is able to spread the word of your brand, yet it is not all about the numbers. It is also the quality of their involvement that counts just as much, or rather more. The affiliates with a good interactive contact with their followers are more prone to create genuine interest in the products they market. That is why it is important to evaluate the activity of potential associates.

Besides, you need an affiliate whose style and content values would appeal to the identity of your brand. Such equivalence increases the validity of the advertising and allows a smooth incorporation of your goods into their works. This way, the affiliate audience will feel that there is a natural association between the products and the materials. They will construct trust, and the likelihood of a conversion being made is higher.

One of the main aspects of affiliate marketing is transparency and authenticity. When affiliates are honest with the products that they use, and when they do not hide their relationships as specialists, then they establish a stronger trust with their followers. Such credibility is manifested in increased conversion rates since consumers would tend to buy what is recommended by a trusted party. Consequently, affiliates who are honest and transparent in their marketing campaigns should be taken into consideration.

The technical strength of affiliates has its share as well. Affiliates that can operate a wide range of tools in the field of digital marketing can end up with highly successful campaigns. This also involves an understanding of analytical tools, which may be helpful in relation to the performance of a campaign, as well as the behavior of people. The affiliates that are able to monitor and optimize their work in real-time can provide added value to your marketing strategy.

Moreover, the terms of partnership have to be beneficial and well-defined between the parties. These involve the choosing of commission, amounts, and frequency of payment, as well as the timeframe of the collaboration. Clear communication and a well-structured agreement will help to avoid misunderstandings in the working relationship and create a positive atmosphere.

In the end, selecting the affiliates must also be done strategically. This involves carrying out proper research and knowing the objectives of your marketing. Choosing affiliates that match your brand values, touch an audience that you wish to pursue, and are prepared to develop adequate technical expertise will enable you to develop a strong affiliate marketing package that will lead to growth and increased awareness of your brand within the online environment.

Tracking and Reporting

The digital marketing world is a complex environment where being able to monitor and report on a set of metrics is key to success. A solid tracking system enables marketers to gain insight into consumer behavior, campaign performance, and the effectiveness of the whole strategy. This is initiated by the identification of key performance indicators (KPIs), which coincide with business goals.

KPIs are a map; they guide marketers on how to determine the outcome of their digital projects.

After the development of KPIs, the next process should be the choice of proper data collection tools and platforms. As an example, Google Analytics is a common tool that offers significant information on the traffic of the sites and behavior of the visitors. Social media networks also provide a native analytics tool, which assists them in monitoring engagement, reach, and conversion numbers. The combination of these tools guarantees an integrated tracking in which data is received through various channels.

The collection of data is just the intro. What is more important is to examine this data and sort out some useful knowledge. It deals with recognizing patterns, trends, and anomalies that could signal the success or failure of some strategies. For example, a sudden increase or decrease in the number of people accessing the site could be caused by a recent promotional effort, and such a change in engagement could also demonstrate the necessity of content optimization.

The next important element is reporting, as it converts raw data in the form of figures, charts, and graphs into a clear story that tells how well the marketing activities worked and reports it to stakeholders. Good reporting must be able to communicate concisely and clearly, as well as analyze the audience. It is rather popular to incorporate visuals, e.g., graphs and charts, to present a trend and a race, thus making difficult information digestible.

In addition, reporting means more than presenting data; rather, reporting involves answering a question in that it is a story of progress where there is an area of improvement. The strategies that are not working and the strategies that are working can be pointed out through regular reports, to lead to informed decision-making. This circular cycle of tracking, analysis, and reporting permits constant reappraisal of marketing strategies and eventually, the realization of a greater performance and the highest return on investment.

Contemporary digital marketing takes into account not only the conventional measures but also more advanced ones like customer journey mapping and attribution modeling. Such methods further improve understanding of the customer journey and allow mapping success back to certain points along the conversion funnel. This comprehension of a full customer journey will allow the marketers to adjust their strategies to target consumer wants and needs to a better extent.

Last but not least, data protection and privacy are important in the tracking and reporting system. Marketers need to be prepared to conform to policies, including the General Data Protection Regulation (GDPR), as data security and privacy become more important. This includes clear data collection methods and permission given by the users, allowing an opinion tracker to monitor their behavior. Ethical treatment of the data is not only a must by the terms of the law, since it helps create confidence among the consumers and is the key to long-term success.

CAMERON BANKS • 101

So, analyzing and reporting about digital marketing is a highly active and continuous procedure and should be approached strategically. With the assistance of the proper tools, data analysis, and the need to be open to the audience, marketers will improve their campaigns, build strong relations with their audience, and achieve their business objectives.

Optimizing Affiliate Efforts

Affiliate marketing is one of the most significant phenomena in digital marketing, providing companies with an accessible and cheap way to project their presence and increase their sales. Optimization of the affiliate work is about the selection and management of affiliate partnerships to make them correspond to the brand and audience needs. The first step of this process involves selecting the possible affiliates whose principles and audiences strike a chord with the brand's spirit and target markets.

Another important part of this optimization is setting up transparent and mutually profitable terms that impel performance and sustain the brand integrity. It is necessary to develop a comprehensive affiliate deal specifying commission percentages, promotional approaches, and performance indicators. This not only creates a definite expectation, but it also creates a transparent and trustful relationship between the affiliates and their brand.

Data analytics is important in perfecting affiliate strategies. Assessing the results of every affiliate in detail allows the businesses to determine the most profitable affiliations. This results-oriented strategy will help marketers to spend resources more effectively by depending on the best-performing affiliates and reconsidering or finishing with the other poor-performing partnerships.

Another point of successful affiliate optimization is the issue of communication. Constant communication with affiliates (in newsletters or during calls with account managers) guarantees that they will have the newest promotional materials and product information. This continues to communicate and keeps the affiliates updated and motivated to deliver superior outcomes to the brand eventually.

Moreover, one can add features to brands to have the best affiliate program, which involves providing affiliates with creative materials and tools that can be utilized to create interesting content. The volume delivery of high-quality images, videos, and ready-made templates will not only help the affiliates in the process of creating an interesting promotion but also guarantee brand consistency across different sources.

Affiliates can also be motivated and incentivized by giving them bonuses or a structure of commissions correlating with performance. These incentives must be in line with defined, attainable goals, which would motivate the affiliates to record even higher levels of performance than in the past. This can be achieved by acknowledging and rewarding the best employees with special incentives or reserved opportunities in order to bring out a competitive but friendly environment.

Nowadays, affiliate strategies have to be constantly innovated in order to remain at the top of the competitive world. This requires keeping up with the industry trends, prescription of modern technologies, and tapping the unexploited market. In such a manner, the businesses will be able to increase the affiliate networks and access new customer groups, which will guarantee consistent development and profitability.

Lastly, the point of legal compliance is the key to maximizing affiliate work. Brands should make sure that their affiliate programmes do not violate any advertising standards or laws. This encompasses giving clear disclosures about the affiliation and making sure that the acts of promotion become legal as per the existing laws.

Affiliate optimisation is not a one-off transaction undertaken, but rather an ongoing exercise that needs a combination of strategic planning, data analysis, and relationship management. With these factors in mind, companies may develop a healthy affiliate relationship to generate revenues and increase brand awareness and reputation within the online market.

CHAPTER 10

MOBILE MARKETING

Understanding Mobile Users

With the advent of mobile technology within the current digital environment, people have been revolutionizing topics of content, services, and brands in the way that they interact with them. Mobile devices are not just another part of our lives; they have become the main source of information, communication, and entertainment. This means that mobile users are the key to the success of businesses and marketers in their efforts to deal with the ever-growing mobile world.

Mobile users can be described as people who lead an on-the-move kind of life and need to access information and avail of services instantaneously. Immediacy and convenience form the core of mobile experience, where the level of intuitive interactions is expected on the side of the user. Mobile subscribers are not chained to a particular place, so they are able to connect even across conventional time and space restrictions. The pervasiveness of this access brings to the fore the necessity of maximizing digital content and interfaces that can be consumed on mobile platforms.

The tendency to use applications and mobile versions of websites with their optimization on a simple, convenient background is another characteristic of mobile users. Such users are used to fast loading times, easy navigation, and compact content that can be read on small screens. Therefore, responsive design and mobile-first approaches have to be the priorities of businesses to satisfy such expectations. Mobile platform skills can have great impacts in the field of consumer satisfaction and brand loyalty due to their capability to give frictionless user experiences.

In addition, mobile users have different behaviour patterns that marketers should take into account. They tend to multitask, and they use their devices during commute, in front of the television, or even when shopping. Such an action creates an effect of shortened attention spans, where shorter and effective content is required to capture interest within the first few seconds. By knowing this, marketers can strategize and therefore send their messages in a manner that the rest will believe in the little period they have of capturing the attention of the user.

The other important thing to note is the diversity of mobile users. Mobile technology use is dependent on age, socioeconomic status, and cultural background. A younger audience, in turn, can be more skilled in using multifunctional app interfaces, whereas older markets will tend to use simplicity and convenience. By identifying these variations, businesses can group their audience efficiently and create exclusive interactions that reflect the individual desires and demands of various user groups.

Moreover, location-based services have emerged because of the existence of mobile devices, and this gives marketers a chance to present extremely accurate and contextual information. With the help of geolocation data, companies will be able to target users with special proposals and inform them about their physical location. Along with the customer experiencing more value, this ability can be used to greater engagement, leading to even more possibilities of conversion.

With the increase in privacy issues, data protection and user consent are complicated issues for mobile users to understand. The attention of mobile users has grown to their digital imprint and the contents they post, so businesses have become adamant about transparent actions and user privacy. To have good relations with mobile audiences, it is mutually critical to establish trust by addressing data responsibility.

To sum it up, mobile users cannot be understood without speaking in a multifaceted language that takes into account the nature of this cogent group, their behavior, and their expectations. Adopting mobile-first approaches, maximizing the user experiences, and taking privacy matters seriously are the right paths to capturing mobile users and catalyzing businesses in the digital era, as well as building relationships with them that may last a long time.

Creating Mobile-Friendly Content

The influence of having mobile-friendly material is difficult to overestimate in the context of digital marketing. With the changes in the technological scene, the recorded trend on how consumers respond to digital content changes requires marketers to modify these approaches. These mobile phones have made people use them as the main way of accessing information, communicating, and even shopping. Thus, producing mobile-friendly content is always an important step towards reaching out to the audience.

First of all, it is important to know about the mobile user behavior. Mobile users have distinctly different needs from most other mobile users as they usually are in flux, and are looking to get simple-to-understand information on the fly. What this implies is that content should be short but meaningful, not too huge so that the reader may be overwhelmed, but should represent what is conveyed. Organizing the material in small paragraphs, using bullets, and strong headings will substantially increase readability on small screens and ensure that the audience will easily navigate the material.

Moreover, visual elements of content are also important in optimizing for mobile use. The images and videos must be resized properly so that they can be loaded without causing a quality decline, since the slow speed of loading can trigger a rise in bounce rates. Also, it is important to make sure that the multimedia content does not ruin the flow of the main content. This entails the tactful use of graphics in a way that they can only be seen as supplements to the written material and not the other way round.

The other pillar of mobile-friendly content creation is the responsive design. The websites and digital tools have to be programmed in such a way that they automatically conform to suit different screen sizes, hence providing an uninterrupted user experience on different devices. This flexibility serves the different varieties of mobile devices. It improves the satisfaction of users in terms of spending more time with the sites, and the probability of them abandoning the sites is low.

In addition to that, mobile-friendly content also relates to search engine optimization (SEO). The search engines, especially Google, favor sites that optimize their web pages for mobile devices. This implies that a website can be adversely affected by the lack of mobile-friendliness, in terms of presence and availability. Some of the practices that are important to stay competitive in digital marketing include mobile-first indexing, which assumes the mobile version of a website to be the main version for indexing and ranking purposes.

Besides, mobile content can also be greatly increased with interactive features. Elements like buttons, which are clicked, interactive infographics, and galleries that can be swiped stimulate the engagement of users better than traditionally static content. Not only do these factors increase interest in the content, but they also encourage users to stay on the site longer, which can increase conversion levels.

Lastly, testing and analytics are inalienable in mobile-friendly content creation. According to this, regular checking of content on different mobile devices should be able to work on different platforms. Understanding how users behave and how they engage gives an idea of what to improve and what is working well, and thus marketers can keep on improving their marketing strategies.

Generating mobile-friendly content is, in essence, the understanding of the specific needs of mobile users and the moulding of digital content to suit the needs of mobile users. Marketers should embrace clarity, responsiveness, and engagement to ensure that they can reach and appeal to their target audience through the ever-growing mobile-shipped digital world.

Mobile App Marketing

Mobile app marketing will be an important element in the context of digital marketing because, in the fast-changing world of digital marketing, mobile application marketing plays a decisive role in terms of attracting the attention of a digitally smart consumer. The traditional concept of marketing has already changed due to the proliferation of smartphones and dependency on mobile applications to perform almost any task, which makes the strategies innovative and adaptive.

Marketing of mobile apps involves several activities aimed at promoting an app through multiple platforms, and the final objective is to gain more downloads, user experience, and retention. The first one is to comprehend the target audience; it should be well known in terms of demographics and behavior of the user in order to create customized marketing techniques. Data analytics allows marketers to understand the preferences of their users and direct the campaign accordingly.

Apple Store Optimization (ASO) is one of the foremost points of mobile app marketing. Similar to the search engine optimization

(SEO) of the sites, ASO is a system that is used to enhance the listing of the app in the app stores in order to make it visible and rank higher in searches. This will entail choosing the appropriate keywords, developing interesting application descriptions, and employing attractive screenshots and video. App store optimization will greatly improve the visibility of the application and get more organic downloads.

Mobile app marketing is of great use as well through social media. Such social media platforms as Facebook, Instagram, and Twitter hold a huge potential audience of billions of users, and opportunities to achieve that are unlike any other. By combining paid promotions and organic content, the marketers will be able to develop captivating campaigns, emphasizing the advantages and peculiarities of the app. These efforts can be further maximized by including influencer deals, which use the credibility and extensive audience of celebrities in the social media realm.

In addition, the scope of mobile app marketing has to take into consideration the whole user journey. The crucial aspect is to ensure that a user remains engaged with the software all the way up to the first download on a routine basis. Push notifications, messages on the app, and corresponding preferences are efficient mechanisms to retain customers and maintain their activity. Nonetheless, marketers should find a balance so that users do not receive excessive notifications that might even result in an app uninstall.

Mobile app marketing is also dependent on retention strategies. By offering a smooth user experience, frequent updates, and new functionality conversions, one can motivate people to use the app even longer. Loyalty programs and gamification elements can be used further to make people use the app more regularly by offering them rewards and fostering further interactions with the app.

Besides the identified strategies, user feedback and reviews are factors that should be used to market mobile apps successfully. Through positive reviews by satisfied users, the reputation of the app can be strengthened to stimulate other users to download the app. A quick and efficient response to negative feedback would indicate commitment to user satisfaction, and it can even make the critics friends.

Last but not least, it is always necessary to measure the effectiveness of mobile app marketing activities in order to continue to improve. The success of marketing is defined by key performance indicators (KPIs), which are the number of downloads, user acquisition cost, the rate of retention, and lifetime value. Through the meaningful study of these measures, the marketers are able to adjust their strategies, spend their resources wisely, and deliver successful results.

Mobile app marketing requires one to be creative, flexible, and highly sensitive to user behaviour in the ever-evolving world of digital marketing. Technology is changing, and never before have marketers faced the need to keep up with trends and stay one step ahead of the problem to keep their apps competitive and in demand in the wide selection of apps in the market.

Analyzing Mobile Metrics

Mobile metrics play a significant role in digital marketing; the knowledge of these metrics can help to be successful and optimize the strategies. The growing popularity of mobile use has changed the relationship consumers have with brands and requires an intense analysis of mobile data to manage and streamline marketing efforts. Mobile metrics are a kind of map that can lead marketers through the sea of consumer behavior and preferences.

Mobile user engagement on different mobile platforms is one of the main elements of mobile metrics analysis. This includes the quantity of user participation with mobile sites and applications, such as the amount of time spent on each site, how often the site is visited, and the amount of interaction. With the help of this analysis, marketers will be able to understand what should be most attractive in their mobile presence and what factors need enhancement.

One more important aspect is measuring the conversion rates on mobile devices. The conversion metrics also enable marketing professionals to learn the success of their mobile programs in creating desired behaviors, including purchasing, registering for a newsletter, etc. The marketers will be able to determine their effective tactics by comparing the conversion rates of the various mobile platforms and campaigns and replicating them in their future marketing campaigns.

Consumer behavior is also very informative in terms of mobile traffic sources. Using the source information of where mobile traffic comes in terms of social media, search engine, and direct traffic, marketers will be able to know which of these sources is the best in reaching the target market. Such knowledge can subsequently be applied to distribute resources more efficiently and to maximize the effect of marketing activities.

Besides, the mobile user demographics analysis will provide a closer insight into the audience. The metrics age, gender, location, and type of device give a complete view of who is reading or listening to mobile content. The demographic information can enable marketers to tailor their messaging and campaigns to be more relevant to the people they are communicating with, hence increasing engagement and conversion.

Another crucial aspect of analysis is the performance of a mobile application. Metrics such as app loading time, crash rate, and user retention can give us an understanding of user experience and show areas for technical enhancement. Marketers will be able to improve the satisfaction of users and create brand loyalty by making sure mobile applications are smooth and efficient.

Also, it is important to understand the effect of mobile advertisement when measuring the success of mobile marketing strategies. One can measure the rate of success of their mobile ads with the help of metrics encompassing click-through rates, cost per click, and return on ad spend, which helps marketers to make informed decisions based on the data available to optimize the advertisement activity.

To conclude, the study of mobile metrics has a multidimensional character. It demands considering diverse information to have a full-scale picture of the behavior of consumers and the success of the campaign. Through the insights, marketers are able to streamline their strategies, enhance user engagement, and eventually attain their marketing objectives. With the still-growing shifts in the digital environment, keeping track of mobile metrics shall be a valuable part of what effective digital marketing methods entail.

CHAPTER 11

VIDEO MARKETING TECHNIQUES

Creating Engaging Videos

Videos have proved to be a powerful force in the field of digital marketing, and they convey more messages with terrific strength and appeal than any other means. Coming up with entertaining videos starts with in-depth knowledge of the intended audience. Having discovered their preferences, interests, and pain points, the latter serve as the fundamental basis on which interesting content is constructed. This consumer-focused attitude makes sure that the videos appeal to the personal level, creating that special feeling and that bond that is both impactful and memorable.

The storyline of the video is the key to avoiding the attrition of the viewer. Proper structure of the story, with a good beginning, middle, and end, directs the viewer to the content logically and interestingly. At the beginning, the viewer should be hooked so that he/she can be led to the message. As the video progresses, there would be a constant flow of information, and there would be no need to have diversions without keeping the viewers concentrated on the main agenda being presented.

The visual component is rather important to make a video interesting. Good visual images and graphics, either in live-action or animation, create a professional, clean appearance. The selection of the dynamic compositions and vivid colors can add emotions and support the message of the video. Also, one may consider adding text overlays and infographics to highlight the most important information further and make it as easy to consume as possible.

Another crucial point of video creation is the sound. The music selection and sound effects may have a remarkably significant effect on the atmosphere and tone of the clip. The music must also go hand in hand with the story, with the aim of enhancing the emotional effect without dominating the dialogue or the image. Spoken audio must be of good quality and clear, so crisp that it does not interfere with even the most visually stimulating video.

It is in editing that the magic occurs. Smooth editing, carefully edited scenes of film, and the sensible employment of effects can help turn raw footage into a smooth and powerful story. Editing is actually a chance to improve the video and make it flawless so that all the seconds play a part in forming the message. It is also the level where timing is mastered, as the beating of the time is just right to make the viewers follow through to the end.

Another trend in the video industry is interactivity, as it is now possible to watch a video interactively. The inclusion of elements like clickable links, quizzes, and polls helps to make such a passive viewing session an active viewing session, resulting in more viewer engagement and retention. The data offered by these interactive factors may also be used to collect information on the preferences and behavior of the audience, and this may be used to design content strategies in the future.

The distribution is important to help extend the reach and influence of a video. Using different platforms, including social media platforms and video hosting sites, among others, guarantees coverage of the content to the desired audience. Every platform has idiosyncratic features and the types of people using the platform, and by customizing to the type of platform, greater effectiveness can be achieved.

Production of a good video is an art and science in this fast-changing world of digital marketing. It also needs creativity and technical expertise, along with the ability to think strategically to create content that not only attracts but also makes people take action. With marketers still experimenting with the website of the possibility of video, the individuals who have perfected the craft of video production will be right at the top of digital innovation.

Video Platforms and Distribution

Video content has become a powerful tool in the sphere of online marketing as it reinforces the concept of brand communications with audiences. The introduction of video networks has created additional opportunities through which marketers can interact with consumers dynamically and interactively. All these platforms, including both YouTube and TikTok, are highly specific, serve different segments of the audience, and engage them in various ways with different expectations.

The power of video content is vindicated by the fact that it is more expressive than the use of text or even images. Visual storytelling is powerful and draws the attention of the viewers in a way that touches them more effectively than conventional advertising can. Brands are turning to video content to strengthen their online presence and boost responses and action.

YouTube has been at the center of video marketing campaigns, and remains so with a huge market and performance analytics at its disposal. Images convey a sense of community, and to leverage this power, brands will use YouTube to upload everything but tutorials, product reviews, and behind-the-scenes recordings to create feelings of authenticity. Such monetization avenues as ads and channel memberships on the platform offer an extra source of revenue to content creators or even brands in general.

The user-generated content model of emerging applications like TikTok has deconstructed video marketing paradigms based on short-form content. The content discovery system used in TikTok, which is mostly algorithm-based, allows brands to capture a wider audience within a shorter time, frequently making its users engage in viral trends and challenges, which help popularize the brands further. Marketers are harnessing the creative opportunity available on TikTok through partnership with influencers and interacting to design content that best speaks to the younger users.

Both Facebook and Instagram remain major areas of video content distribution, and both have introduced features such as stories and IGTV, which encourage users to publish their activities spontaneously and naturally. These media also enable brands to reach their patrons by creating interactive live streams and options, encouraging immediate interaction and response. Another way streaming on these platforms makes the process of getting through the path to purchase easier is by integrating the functions of shopping into the video content.

The emergence of live streaming has also opened up video marketing to new opportunities. Real-time content delivery like Twitch and Facebook Live has become more popular, and real-time delivery platforms can allow brands to host live events, Q&A sessions, and product launches. Through live streaming, the concept of immediacy and sense of community is created where viewers can directly interact with brands and influencers.

Video content distribution is an issue that needs to be addressed strategically with consideration of the peculiarities of every platform and the target audience. Marketers need to manipulate their information to suit the platform trends and behaviours and ensure that they match the content to the target audience. Moreover, data analytics is essential to the optimization of video content strategies, with in-depth insights concerning the viewers' preferences and performance metrics.

Video platforms will certainly become part and parcel of marketing strategies as the digital space continues to develop. The flexibility of utilizing the latest technologies and audience tastes will be crucial in taking full advantage of video material. When brands manage to negotiate this volatile environment, they will be able to get the attention and loyalty of their target groups easily.

Live Streaming Strategies

Live streaming has become an incredible weapon to be used in digital marketing, which implies the active maintenance of contact with the audience to interact with them in real-time. Through the use of this technology, brands have been able to establish genuine ties with their market, providing them with an immediate and interactive touch unlike other media.

Live streaming requires having a clear profile of the target audience and the goals of the broadcast to be able to make sound use of this feature. The determination of these parameters contributes to the creation of content that will be welcomed by viewers and make the live stream useful and worth attention. This includes the choice of topics that are relevant to the audience, either in terms of product launch, behind the scenes, or a live Q&A session.

The technical side of live streaming is also a very important factor behind its success. A stable internet connection, quality of audio and video, and an appropriate streaming platform are the key aspects that add to the smooth watching process. These components need to be tested before the system is put live in order to avoid technical hitches, which may interrupt the transmission.

Interactivity is the key to an effective live stream. By suggesting viewers to comment, ask questions, and participate in polls, it is possible not only to keep the audience entertained but also to learn a lot about their likes and dislikes. There is a sense of community and the connection achieved by responding to the inputs of the audience in real-time, which makes the experience really personal and memorable.

Another essential measure is marketing the live stream beforehand. Using different digital platforms, including social media, email newsletters, and websites, to create awareness of the upcoming event will aid in creating anticipation and thus a higher turnout. Bright or clear communication of a date and time of a live stream and the platform that will be used to reach the highest number of people is important.

Post-broadcast techniques are also significant in spreading the effects and coverage of the live broadcast. Showing the session later and on demand will enable people who were not in attendance during the airing of the event to view it whenever they want. Also, viewer statistics may be analyzed to give insight as to how the audience behaves and their interests, which can be used in future live streaming plans.

The inclusion of the elements of storytelling in the live stream can contribute to its popularity immensely. Emotional or emotional stories may be used; stories that are interesting to follow may help one capture the attention of the audience and thus be remembered better. It is a strategy that not only deepens interaction but also makes the brand message and image stronger.

Moreover, partnerships with influencers or other professionals in the field of livestreaming can help reach a greater number of people and give credibility to the video. These collaborations have the potential to bring on board new viewers, who might not have heard about the brand before, hence making the number of viewers even larger.

Keeping up with the latest trends and technological advances in live streaming is important, as digital landscapes are still constantly developing. The ease of adaptation to new tools and platforms may be used as a competitive advantage and ensure that the brand stays at the forefront of innovations in the field of digital marketing. Constant development of live streaming approaches enables brands to be relevant and successfully reach their audience in the ever-evolving digital environment.

Measuring Video Success

Videos have also turned out to be a necessity of digital marketing in reaching the audience, as well as presenting a message in a motion picture form. It is imperative to gauge the success of the video content to tap its potential to the best. This would include knowing different metrics and analytics that allow for an understanding of how well a video is doing and how it contributes to higher marketing objectives.

View count is one of the key parameters that one should monitor, as it shows the number of times a video is viewed. Whereas a large number of views may indicate popularity, this may not imply effectiveness. We have to look deeper into audience participation, which will determine the success. It entails the evaluation of watch time or the duration that viewers remain logged in. The increased amount of time spent watching usually indicates that the video is interesting and keeps the audience engaged.

It is also essential to measure the success of videos with the help of engagement data like likes, shares, and comments. Such communications give a hint of how well the material may or may not relate to the audience and are a way of getting the mood or flavor of the audience. Shares are of special significance because they can increase the scope of the video to those not included in its original viewership. Comments include qualitative information, which may bring out the opinion of viewers, and they will offer helpful feedback regarding future content production.

The other important metric is the click-through rate (CTR), which determines the number of times that a viewer clicks on a call-to-action (CTA), which is embedded in a video. High CTR means that the video is useful in encouraging viewers to complete the specific action, which can be a visit to the bookmarked address, subscription to the newsletter, or buying a product. It is also necessary to track the conversion, i.e., measure the number of viewers who will take the intended action, to determine the effect of video on business goals.

Another useful metric is the retention rate, or the number of viewers who watch the video till the finish. It assists in knowing the point of falling off when the viewers lose interest. Through this analysis, marketers would be able to improve their content in order to keep their audiences engrossed with the video throughout.

Moreover, one should remember the context in which the video is watched. The metrics shall be tracked together with demographic data to identify who is viewing a video and whether it is delivered to the target market. This entails factors like age, gender, location, and viewing devices, which are all capable of altering the content consumption and perception.

Knowledge of these metrics can provide marketers with the possibility of optimizing video content, making strategies audience-oriented, and end up with more successful marketing campaigns using video. Through constant evaluation of performance resources, marketers will be able to make the correct judgment and readjust their strategies to optimum engagement and reach marketing goals. The knowledge gleaned in terms of determining the success of videos cannot be underestimated in terms of improving the strategies used to produce content and in making video a force to reckon with in the digital marketing arsenal.

CHAPTER 12

WEB ANALYTICS AND DATA INTERPRETATION

Understanding Web Analytics

Web analytics are the core of online marketing, offering information about user behavior, preferences, and their interactions in the online platform. This thorough examination helps them to interpret the huge mass of information created by users through accessing websites and digital content. Using web analytics, companies are able to monitor and analyze important performance indicators, which are essential in the optimization of the marketing process and the improved user experience.

Web analytics, in its basic form, entails the process of gathering, measuring, and interpreting information on the web to gain knowledge of the same and streamline web use. The whole point of this process is not to gather information but to turn it into useful insights ready to inform the decision-making and strategy development process. The metrics that might be obtained in web analytics include page views, unique visitors, bounce rate, conversion rate, and user demographics, among others.

Among the seminal advantages of web analytics is the fact that it gives an in-depth insight into the visiting experience of consumers concerning a page. This data on interactions can provide patterns and tendencies that can enable marketers to determine which content or feature is most appealing to the users. As an example, through monitoring the most heavily trafficked pages or the routes that visitors may follow on the Internet, companies will be in a position to maximize user engagement and retention.

In addition to this, web analytics tools have the potential to make businesses aware of their marketing activities. Marketers are able to measure the effectiveness of their campaigns by identifying sources of their traffic, conversion rates, and user engagement, as well as detailing areas of improvement to their strategy. Such a data-driven strategy can lead to greater targeted marketing, as no effort goes to waste and generates a maximum of returns.

The other important feature of web analytics is the fact that it is used to improve the user experience. Businesses can customize their websites according to the requirements and expectations of their customers by learning user behavior. This may include navigation enhancement of interfaces, increasing page responsiveness, or customization to boost user experience and satisfaction.

Moreover, web analytics can be used to get useful data on customer demographics and psychographics that help businesses to have a better view and knowledge of who they serve. This knowledge could be used to implement more customized marketing approaches and campaigns that appeal to different categories of customers.

Alongside such advantages, web analytics is also significant in aspects such as competition analysis. With the help of industry trends and the analysis of competitor performance, businesses will also be able to see the opportunity in relation to differentiation and growth. This competitive intelligence can inform strategic planning, and the business involved can get ahead of the fast-changing environment in the digital age.

Generally, web analytics serves as a handy tool for digital marketers and presents a treasure of information that would help a business to grow and thrive. Systematic analysis of web data enables business owners to make informed decisions, which can increase their strategy effectively with regard to marketing, user experience, and overall objectives. The difference between unsuccessful and successful web analytics is the ability to properly interpret the information and use it in the right way that will comply with the business needs and meet customer demands.

Setting Up Analytics Tools

In order to initiate the process of appropriate implementation of analytics tools, it is necessary to understand, first of all, the spirit of the goals of the business and how they are combined with the whole concept of digital marketing. Identification of key performance indicators (KPIs) that will give an idea of whether the marketing campaigns are successful should be done. Those KPIs are targets that can be used to monitor improvement and make decisions.

It is imperative to find the right analytics platforms. Companies have to consider several different tools in the market, including Google Analytics and Adobe Analytics, or decide on the use of specialized software depending on the industry in which they operate or on the particular requirement. The platforms have individual characteristics, and one should pay attention to such factors to choose the best platform, as the complexity of ease of use, its ability to integrate, price, and the possibility of scale.

After selecting a fitting analytics tool, the following step is to adjust it to monitor appropriate data. It occurs when tracking codes or pixels are used on the site or the mobile applications. These codes must be placed correctly because they will determine the reliability of the data obtained. Many times, the business might require collaborating with developers and IT people to apply these technical aspects properly.

Another critical factor is the customization of the analytics dashboard. The customization of the dashboard allows companies to put more emphasis on the most important gauges, hence concentrating on information that really counts in achieving the objectives. Such tailoring involves the establishment of reports and alerts to inform the stakeholders concerning any substantial changes or patterns in the data.

Segments in the analytics tools cannot be set up without enlightening the target audience. Segmentation enables companies to study the behaviors and preferences of various classes of clients. Such insight is capable of guiding even more specific and effective approaches to marketing since companies can target their messages to be more appealing to certain groups of audiences.

Inaccurate and compromised data is unacceptable. Regularly auditing the data collection process would help detect and make corrections in case of any discrepancy. The fact that the data that is under analysis would be clean and correct would help avoid misleading conclusions and aid more reliable decision-making.

Analytics platforms can be complemented with other tools in marketing. By incorporating analytics and CRM platforms, email marketing, or social media advertising tools, companies will have a better picture of their marketing. This end-to-end planning facilitates more strategic planning.

It is also essential to train and empower team members to use analytics tools. With detailed training sessions and materials, everyone will be able to analyse the data well and make quality decisions. Adoption of a data-driven culture in the organization will lead to a proactive attitude toward the maximization of marketing strategies.

Regular observation and updating are crucial for sustaining the functionality of analytics applications. The analytics setup should therefore match the level at which the businesses are growing and evolving. Periodically rebalancing and adjusting the configuration makes sure that it constantly serves the shifting requirements of the business.

With the help of a thorough implementation of analytics tools by taking such considerations into account, the company can unveil the secrets that lead to flourishing and find the greatest way of improving its digital marketing strategy. Such a meticulous approach to the process of setting up forms the basis of data-driven decision-making and strategic success within the digital environment.

Interpreting Data

Data is used as the basis of informed decision-making in the digital marketing field. Knowing how to decipher this data is extremely important to marketers who are interested in improving strategies and maximizing campaigns. Interpreting data is not only an exercise of identifying the patterns and trends but also attaching context and implications of the information to future marketing actions.

First, data is a word that should be well understood in terms of the various types of data that marketers can use. They are in the forms of quantitative data, which is numerical and can be measured, and also qualitative data, which is descriptive and is characterized by more subjective analysis. Quantitative measures may involve measures of conversion, click-throughs, and ROI, whereas qualitative information may involve customer reviews and brand sentiment.

Quantitative data analysis is conducted using statistical techniques in order to find connections and trends. This could involve the application of program packages to perform regression analysis, cluster analysis, or predictive modeling. The techniques prevent marketers from knowing how the various aspects affect their campaigns the most and how other parts of the campaign communicate with each other. To give another example, regression analysis of data can help a marketer realize that the increase or decrease in the amount of ad spending relates directly to the increase or decrease in the level of customer engagement.

On the contrary, the qualitative data requires another approach. Analysis of this kind of data frequently includes thematic analysis in which data is coded into themes or patterns. This may entail being able to read through customer reviews and get the general feelings or thoughts about a product or service. Numerical insights obtained after quantitative analysis can be combined with the insights obtained after qualitative data, and really give a complete picture of customer behavior and inclination.

Another very important element, when interpreting data, is context. In the case of consumers, marketers need to take into account external influences that may change data trends, e.g., changes in the economy, seasonal changes, and transformation of consumer behaviour. Like, a rise in online sales over a specific period may not necessarily be pegged as a result of a well-organized marketing campaign, but it may also be due to the influence of holiday shopping or variation in consumer buying power.

Additionally, data interpretation is not a single event, and it is an ongoing procedure. Marketers should always keep track of the numbers to be able to see and respond to emerging trends. This flexible model enables the marketer to be sensitive to environmental changes and readjustments in consumer behavior so that his/her marketing endeavor is appropriate and receptive.

Information visualization is also very important in the interpretation of data. The conversion of complex datasets into a visual type, such as charts, graphs, or a dashboard, helps marketers to distinguish a trend more easily and convey the results of the findings to stakeholders. In addition to facilitating the process of interpretation, effective data visualization can also improve data-driven decision making.

Effectively, data interpretation in digital marketing would amount to a combination of analytical ability, context, and constant observation. Through adequate interpretation of data, marketers will be able to extract important insights on consumer behavior, streamline their strategies, and eventually yield better results in business. Interpretation of data, therefore, constitutes a critical tool of any digital marketer who is eager to succeed in the current data-intensive environment.

Using Data for Decision Making

In digital marketing, information presents itself as a valuable tool, as it influences the decisions to be made and shapes the first steps the companies are to take on their way to reaching their target market groups. Needless to say, the role of data in decision-making is paramount, the key to the success of the marketing strategy. Through the analysis of data, marketers are able to achieve a deep level of knowledge in consumer behavior, likes, and trends; thus, one is able to campaign in a precise and efficient manner.

Data gathering is the first step, and all the gathered data can be found through a broad variety of sources, including web analytics, social media feedback, customer responses, and sales. Each item of information is a puzzle and will help to create a bigger image of the consumer scene. The information is then analyzed carefully to get patterns and see what may not be clear at a glance. Highly sophisticated analytical systems and computer programmes also come in very handy during this stage, as they enable marketers to filter a lot of information.

When the data has been analyzed, it is an effective tool for drawing informed decisions. As an example, the knowledge of the marketing channel that will give them the best return on their investments can help businesses manage their resources better. Equally, customer preference will be used to develop products and advertisement efforts since it will be known how it should be done to suit customers.

Besides, data-driven decision making leads to a higher predictive power of occurrence and consumer patterns, which enables businesses to keep ahead of the curve. Through predictive analytics, marketers will be able to know changes that will happen in the market and also adjust accordingly. Such an offensive strategy will not only make the businesses more competitive but also lead them to become innovative, since companies are always trying to find new methods to deal with the changing requirements of their consumers.

The other important feature of data use in decision making is that it enables one to personalize marketing initiatives. Data helps marketers to reveal the paths of the individual customer and hence have the ability to design a more personalized experience. Therefore, it connects with the consumer in a deeper sense. Such personalization may highly boost client engagement and loyalty, because an individual is more prone to reacting well to the message being conveyed to them when such messages are aligned with their interests and needs.

There are, however, challenges associated with the use of data. It is critical to have quality and useful information, with erroneous information raising the possibilities of inaccurate decisions that may result in inappropriate planning and wastage of resources. Furthermore, companies have to wade through the waters of data privacy and safety, and consumer information should be used with responsibility and an ethical approach.

Data has to be learnt to be used as part of the decision-making process. Hence, a cultural change needs to be embraced in the context of the organization, with data literacy being an imperative aspect at all levels. Employees can be enabled to exploit the power of data through training and development programs that help them think in terms of data, and such a culture should permeate the organization.

Finally, decision-making with the strategic use of data is an evolving thing, but an active one. It should be watched and adjusted constantly when new information is forthcoming and when the circumstances in the market are changing. Incorporating a data-driven culture can help businesses optimize marketing, generate growth, and become successful in the long term in the dynamic digital world.

CHAPTER 13

DIGITAL MARKETING AUTOMATION

Introduction to Automation Tools

Digital marketing remains a dynamic field that changes continuously as new technologies emerge, and most businesses need automation instruments to achieve the desired efficiency and streamline their processes. Such tools will be used to support routine activities, such that marketers will concentrate on strategic planning and creative activities. Automation within digital marketing includes a myriad of capabilities; email marketing and managing social media, analytics, and customer relationship management are but a few.

Automation tools help marketers to run campaigns accurately and consistently as they work to make sure that the right message gets to the audience at the most opportune time. These tools will enable businesses to target their marketing as a result of using data and analytics to come up with targeted marketing messages, which will enable businesses to address the right audience and make a positive impact. Such customization not only enhances the customer experience but also leads to increased conversion.

Among the principal benefits of automation tools is time and resource saving. Businesses can direct part of their workforce to more significant duties since the automation of routine functions enables companies to achieve greater productivity. As an example, automated email marketing platforms can be used to pre-determine and send automatic emails that reach large numbers of subscribers without physically touching them. On the same note, management tools in social media may assist in scheduling posts, monitoring engagement, and developing a more effective marketing strategy.

In addition to that, the automation tools also give useful data by bringing up superior information collected and analyzed. They enable marketers to track the progress of the campaign in real-time, which permits them to shift strategies to suit the required changes. This technique of using data will allow the marketing activity to improve progressively. Through customer behavior and preferences, companies will be able to perfect their products and services. They will be able to align their marketing messages to the changing demands of their customers.

Besides efficiency and data understanding, automation tools improve scalability. These tools have the advantage of being able to cope with an increase in demand as businesses expand. This scalability plays a significant role in consistency in marketing campaigns, irrespective of the number of audiences involved in the marketing campaigns and the complexity of operations.

The new use of automation tools in digital marketing approaches contributes to the cooperation between the team members. With the ability to host the centralized platform to manage campaigns, such tools make sure that every member of the team can see the same information, and it is possible to coordinate the work and minimize the risks of miscommunication. Such a channel of collaboration is therefore crucial in the effective implementation of thorough-going marketing plans.

In addition, automation software is constantly improving, and now it includes sophisticated technologies like artificial intelligence and machine learning. Such innovations make even higher customization and efficiency feasible, as the businesses will be able to forecast the conduct of the customers and personalize their marketing campaigns accordingly. With the development of these technologies, automated tools will only be able to provide an increased number of options for advancing innovation in digital marketing.

To sum up, automation tools play a crucial role in contemporary digital marketing. These not only establish efficiency and boost productivity, but they also give the insight and scalability to make effective marketing initiatives successful. With the rise of businesses in the digital world, automation tools are the best way to remain in the competitive business environment in the long run.

Workflow Automation

Workflow automation is one of the highlighted factors in digital marketing when it comes to the promotion of efficiency and productivity in the constantly changing scenery of internet marketing.

It is a tool that helps to carry out duplicating businesses in a more streamlined manner, thereby enabling marketers to focus on more strategic matters. In essence, workflow automation is the application of technology to perform the repeated processes or activities within the marketing workflow, to which manual labor may be substituted.

Automation tools are planned to administer convoluted marketing campaigns in a variety of channels in such a way that each aspect of the marketing campaign is done at the correct time and in the appropriate order. It entails the installation of triggers and procedures that lead to automation. As an example, once a potential customer subscribes to a newsletter, it is possible to set up an automated workflow, which would automatically send a welcome email, add the user to a mailing list, and even send a follow-up email in a few days. These types of systems not only save time but also provide consistency and precision in marketing attempts.

A better revolution in adopting machine learning and artificial intelligence in the automation of workflow processes has also changed how marketers perform their duties. These technologies allow systems to train on inputs of data and make informed decisions without human input. To give one example, an automation tool that uses AI may be able to track the actions of customers to identify their future trends so that marketers can adapt their strategies to suit those habits.

In addition, the automation of work helps to manage resources better. Teams are free to spend their time and effort on more innovative and effective projects that are carried out due to the automation of routine tasks. This transition not only makes work better but also gives better quality marketing campaigns. Instead of being overwhelmed by administrative tasks, teams could focus on the development of new strategies and interesting content.

The capability of workflow automation to offer informative analytics is another major point. Automated systems can trace and report on different measures in real-time, which would provide quality information on the performance of the campaigns. This information would enable marketers to perfect their plans, allocate resources efficiently, and eventually build stronger performance.

Although this kind of work is associated with many benefits, automation of workflows should be planned and thought out. It is important to sketch current outcomes and design the workflows that may best be automated. This is a process that necessitates the knowledge of the complexities of each task and how automation is going to increase efficiency without sacrificing quality.

Moreover, the move to an automated system may be problematic, including failure by team members who have grown accustomed to carrying out manual procedures. Thus, proper training and assurance should be given so that it is a smooth transition. Explaining the advantages and possibilities of automation would facilitate the buy-in of all stakeholders.

On the whole, work automation is an essential element of the digital marketing strategy. It allows marketers to accomplish more personal and timely communications, to coordinate their resources in better ways, and achieve the potential of having continuous, better-performing campaigns. With the future of workflow automation only becoming more and more ambitious, it is clear that the possibilities of this technology are going to seem even larger and more promising due to the needs and changes in the sphere of digital marketing.

Personalization and Automation

In the busy digital marketing field, where innovative technologies change the rules of the game even on a daily basis, the synergy of personalization and automation becomes one of the key aspects that alters the standards of interaction between businesses and their audience. The combination of these two elements provides marketers with a chance to customize experiences and accelerate processes, thus improving customer interaction and business effectiveness.

Digital marketing consumes personalization by creating personal messages and a personal experience directed towards a specific customer. With the help of data analytics and consumer insight, marketers would be able to break down their audience's behaviors, preferences, and demographics, making them not only relevant but interesting as well. Such a strategy goes beyond the conventional one-size-fits-all approach that enables companies to get closer to consumers. The effect of personalization is quite extensive; the element builds brand loyalty, boosts the conversion rate, and eventually facilitates sales.

Automation, instead, uses technology to perform tasks with little human intervention. Repetitive tasks that automation tools can be used in digital marketing are email marketing, social media posting, and ad campaigns. In the automation of the processes, marketers will have time to engage in strategic planning and creative activities. Automation leads to time saving, consistency, and accuracy in the applications of marketing strategies.

It is at the crossroads of personalization and automation that the real innovation lies. Machine learning algorithms based on AI can be applied to analyze huge amounts of data to detect patterns and trends so that personalized marketing efforts can be developed. A good example is that an e-commerce site may find use in automating messages or suggestions to different customers on what they can purchase, depending on their browsing history and purchasing patterns. This improves both the buying process and the chances of buying the same product again.

Further, chatbot innovation is one example of how personalization and automation can go hand in hand. These artificial intelligence-based tools are able to interact with customers in real-time and can offer individual help and responses whenever necessary, 24/7. The use of chatbots can guide and process requests, product recommendations, and even transactions, making the customer experience smooth and personalized, and at the same time, efficient.

Nonetheless, consumer data use should be ethical and considerate in order to make personalization and automation work. The marketers are required to be transparent and keep the consumers informed of their beliefs by following the laws of data protection and privacy norms. Finding a balance between using information to personalize and not invading the privacy of consumers has been imperative to developing sustainable and trustworthy relationships with consumers.

Personalization and automation do not go hand in hand in digital marketing, but they are imperative to implement. With the ever-increasing consumer demands, companies that cannot embrace such strategies would lag. The future of digital marketing is creating individual experiences in a mass market, which is only achievable due to the capabilities of automated systems, which are also very malleable to the changing market forces.

In this way, by combining personalization and automation, marketers can generate more valuable connections with their consumers and, hence, prompt engagement and instigate loyalty. With the ever-changing world of technology, the scope of personalization and automations in digital marketing is limitless, and we will soon find in the future that marketing plans will be continuously evolving to a new level and as unique as the customers they are targeting.

Evaluating Automation Success

Automation tools in digital marketing. When it comes to digital marketing, using automation tools offers an opportunity to improve effectiveness and efficiency. The most important question that emerges as business applications of these technologies rise is how business success can be realized adequately. Measuring the success of automation cannot be reduced to one single point in time; instead, it presupposes a multidimensional analysis, which takes into account not only the current results but also long-term strategic value.

At the centre of this evaluation are the apprehension of key performance indicators (KPIs) that resonate with the strategic high-level objectives of the marketing strategy. These KPIs are indicators of gauging the effects of automation tools on marketing campaigns. As an example, ratios of sales, lead generation, conversion, customer engagement, and returns on investment (ROI) could be used to identify the real value of automation for a business. All these metrics can provide information regarding various campaign processes, which include attracting potential customers and transforming them into regular customers.

The quantitative measures of automation are not the only ones significant: the qualitative measures assess their success aptly. These comprise knowledge on customer satisfaction and feedback, which gives an in-depth perception of the influence of automation on customers. The response can be collected using surveys, direct contact, and observing social media, which provides a broad view of customer perception. This qualitative data will be able to show places where automation is going well and where it could use some improvement.

The other significant element of the discussion of the success of automation is its assimilation into the current systems and processes. Integration becomes seamless, and automation tools should not create disturbances since they should be used to augment the already existing workflow. There is a need to evaluate their compatibility with the available software, databases, and communication media. Correct integration will result in more accurate data, efficient operations, and better teamwork, which can be used to have a more solid marketing strategy.

Additionally, it is critical to review the versatility and extensibility of automation tools. What happens when businesses expand and the markets become dynamic, providing new challenges? This is critical since the size of these tools would determine how well they perform in the longer term. This entails the determination of whether the tools would be able to accommodate larger volumes of data, more functions, and incorporate new technologies as they are developed.

Besides, the human factor in automation achievement cannot be disregarded. The success of automation usually depends on the possibility of its use by the marketing team. The productivity that training team members can achieve will be improved, and will increase innovation, through upskilling to leverage automation technology. The simplicity of these tools, vendor support, and continuous training resources for the employees should also be taken into account.

Finally, one should consider the cost-benefit of the automation tools. Short-term investments could cost a lot; however, the long-term savings and the level of revenue that could be generated afterwards should cover such investments. Companies must carry out a cost-benefit analysis, so that the amount of money they invest in automation will eventually be worth much later.

Measuring the effectiveness of marketing automation is a complex process that takes into consideration quantitative and qualitative indicators, integration and scalability, as well as human communication and economic feasibility. All these factors offer useful points that give information on the general success of automation tactics, and this should be used to shape and gear up digital marketing activities by businesses.

CHAPTER 14

FUTURE TRENDS IN DIGITAL MARKETING

Emerging Technologies

Technological changes in digital marketing realms are significantly transforming how firms relate to their consumers in the fast-changing environment. Marketers who want to remain competitive and relevant have no choice but to embrace emerging technologies in their integration. Such technologies are disrupting the old marketing techniques and allowing more personalised, efficient, and data-driven techniques.

In the center of such a technological revolution is Artificial Intelligence (AI). Machine learning, natural language processing, and predictive analytics, which are AI technologies, are helping marketers to process huge data volumes to obtain information about consumer behavior and preferences. This can be used to establish very specific advertising campaigns that are able to appeal to individual customers. Chatbots and virtual assistants that are implemented with the help of AI also complement the work done by customer service, as they can work 24/7 and contribute to customer satisfaction.

The other important technology that is making a difference in digital marketing is Augmented Reality (AR). AR is creating immersive and interactive consumer experiences, and it is changing the way products are being presented. The technology enables customers to see products within the setting of their environment prior to making purchases, thus cutting down uncertainties and boosting the rate of conversion. As an example, furniture stores are applying AR to allow consumer to experience the appearance of a piece of furniture in their living room, such as Kiks Furniture stores.

The sphere of digital marketing also experiences the flow of blockchain technology. Cryptocurrency is the most popular project that has been secured using blockchain technology. Because the blockchain is transparent and decentralised, it is being used to give a higher level of security to the data that is exchanged and establish some form of a trust relationship between the consumer and the company. This technology is especially useful in fighting ad fraud in a way that allows digital advertising to be delivered to the target. In addition to that, blockchain will be able to ensure more transparent and secure transactions, which will be essential in developing trust between consumers and brands.

Another game-changer is the Internet of Things (IoT), which links a range of devices and makes it possible to gather real-time data. This connection enables marketers to learn about the interaction with their products in a new way that has never been experienced before. The IoT devices can help reveal how products are utilized, and thus the brands have a chance to improve their products and make them more personalized, or in other words, have better marketing plans.

Digital marketing is also affected by voice search technology. As the number of smart speakers and voice-activated gadgets grows, it is increasingly crucial to optimize the content for voice search. This is done by learning how to use conversational language and how it should be formatted to fit the manner in which people ask questions verbally. Subsequently, voice search is restructuring SEO and content development as it continues to expand.

Furthermore, marketing is encouraging more informed decision-making that is being fueled by big data analytics. The capability to process huge data enables marketers to recognize the trends, evaluate the campaigns, and predict future consumer patterns. More efficient marketing strategies and resultant ROI are the outcomes of this data-driven approach.

Such new technologies do not merely imply having new tools; rather, they are the impetus of innovation in digital marketing. They are helping marketers to develop more personalized, exciting, and more efficient sales campaigns that are able to satisfy emerging consumer demands. With the technologies becoming more advanced, their usage in marketing strategies is bound to change the face of digital marketing, putting new opportunities and challenges before marketers across the globe.

AI in Marketing

Artificial intelligence (AI) has become one of the defining factors of such a fast-changing environment of digital marketing, reinventing business interactions with its audiences. The tools of AI technology, including processing large volumes of data and learning patterns, provide marketers with new possibilities unheard of in terms of improving their approaches and approaching a more personalized interaction with customers.

The ability to analyze consumer behaviour and predict future trends is perhaps one of the greatest things that AI has brought to marketing. Using machine learning algorithms, marketers have an opportunity to learn more about what customers like and adjust their campaigns to their tastes. Such an approach, based on the collection of data, makes it possible to develop very targeted marketing messages appealing to that segment of the audience, which promotes more engagement and higher conversion rates.

AI is also important in the automation of repetitive tasks, and this liberates the precious time that marketers need so that they can concentrate on other strategic tasks. Automation enables the handling of things like email marketing, social media posting, and even interaction with customers, and all these can be done efficiently without compromising on quality. Examples of AI-based chatbots involve assisting customers in real-time, answering their questions, and solving their problems at an efficiency scale that human agents may hardly be able to compete with.

Another place where AI has significantly impacted is personalization. AI systems are capable of recommending custom content and products, including dynamic pricing models, due to the data collected at touchpoints. Such a high degree of personalization allows not only to improve the customer experience but also to build brand loyalty through the feeling of customer appreciation and understanding.

Additionally, analytics tools powered by AI allow marketers to identify how effective their campaigns are more accurately. Through real-time data analysis and key performance indicator (KPI) tracking, marketers can formulate real-time decisions and, therefore, change their approach to their strategies. This swiftness comes in handy at a time when the digital era has created a situation where the whims and fancies of customers may suddenly take a new direction, and only keeping up-to-date can help to gain a competitive advantage.

The process of creativity in the field of marketing is also evolving due to the use of AI. AI algorithms are advanced and able to come up with content ideas, develop ads, and even come up with music tracks or write articles, giving a new toolbox to marketers who want to develop their creative work. Although human creativity is something that cannot be replaced with anything, artificial intelligence can be used in the creative process to provide a new insight and to make the process of artificial creativity less time-consuming.

Even when many benefits of using AI in marketing are listed, its incorporation is not a challenge-free process. The issue of data privacy and ethical concerns should be resolved to make sure the use of AI applications is responsible. Marketers should also consider the possibility of AI being a carrier of the biases that the training data may include, and causing biased insight and decision-making.

The prospect of AI in marketing is immense, and more and more developments in technology should contribute to its improvement. With its increased involvement in marketing plans, it is safe to assume that those companies that have embraced AI and utilized its capabilities to the full will feel its substantial rewards in terms of efficiency, customer satisfaction, and, in general, brand prosperity. It is all about finding a middle ground between technological advances and human wisdom, where AI is implemented not to do the human parts of the marketing but to supplement them.

The Rise of Voice Search

Over the past couple of years, the digital marketing scene has undergone a radical shift due to the introduction of voice search technology. Since the rise of smart speakers and virtual assistants will extend to even more homes and workplaces, there is a massive change in how consumers search for information. This development is not only a technological change but also a pure shift in user behaviour, and it requires marketers to evolve and change their approach to things.

The use of such devices as Amazon Echo, Google Home, or Apple Siri has created the popularity of voice search as a convenient feature that allows users to find a solution without touching their devices. The possibility of voice search to answer the questions immediately, to make the process smooth, and not to be compared to text searches is its magic. This ease of use is especially useful in cases when the user needs to multitask, like in making food, driving, or working out, where the regular method of typing and browsing falls short.

The voice search is on a different plane from normal search engines. It is more based on natural language processing, and it has allowed users to communicate with the technology naturally. The evolution of search queries to a more conversational form implies that search algorithms will have to be developed with the ability to grasp and utilize longer and more complex questions, as well as closely resemble those that human beings would use when addressing one another in dialogue. This has tasked the marketers with the obligation of ensuring that their content can be optimized to such conversational keywords, which most of the time cannot be very similar to the text-based ones.

The voice search has enormous repercussions on digital marketing. Among the most profound changes, the emphasis on local search optimization should be listed. Most voice queries are local, and therefore, companies need to make sure that their online presence is geared towards local customers. This also involves proper management of correct and valid information on listing platforms such as Google My Business, as well as search optimisation of the issue of the near me searches, since these searches have become rather common.

In addition to that, the emergence of voice search is affecting content development strategies. The new trend in marketing is to formulate content that provides direct question-and-answer responses, as in most questions associated with voice search. This not only entails integration of the relevant keywords but also a more conversational language that is in line with the language the user uses. The significance of featured snippets, or, as they are also known, position zero results, has increased as well, since these are the answers that voice assistants usually give.

Consumer expectations are also being formed as voice search technology is evolving. Customers are getting used to the idea of having solo-mixed responses that are in line with their tastes and previous affairs. This shift is causing marketers to embrace outcomes of data analytics and machine learning to create more customized and personalized experiences. Identifying the user intent and context is increasingly becoming critical, enabling brands to pre-empt and directly serve the context and find solutions.

The emergence of voice search may be seen to pose a challenge, but also has a chance of innovation. Those brands that incorporate this technology and align their strategy with its use will obtain a competitive advantage in the online market. With the emphasis on the improvement of user experience and the delivery of both valuable and easy-to-access information, companies can establish closer relationships with their customers.

When we look ahead, further assimilation of voice technology in our lives is bound to happen. This development will probably cause even greater artificial intelligence and machine learning, and the development of even deeper interactions with the products by consumers. To marketers, it will be important to get ahead of such trends and decipher the dynamics of voice search in the shifting world of online platforms.

Sustainability in Digital Marketing

Sustainability has become a central topic in digital marketing as it has resulted in the general growth being more environmentally oriented. This chapter takes a deeper look into the complex connection between sustainability and digital marketing, showing how companies can integrate their marketing efforts with a sustainable organizational approach in a way that not only improves the image of the business but also brings good to the environment.

The use of technology and the internet framework is inherent in digital marketing, which means that this marketing option uses resources and energy. However, it presents a special kind of value in the form of promoting sustainable activities through its reach and presence. When using digital platforms, companies may promote environmental awareness and initiate pro-ecological consumer behavior. An example is that businesses can use social media campaigns to portray their sustainability efforts, like cutting carbon footprints or contributing to renewable energy efforts.

In addition, digital marketing helps to do efficient and targeted communication, eliminating the use of such marketing materials as print advertising or brochures that cause deforestation and leave waste behind. Switching to online means companies will be able to reduce their environmental footprint tremendously. This change will not only be sustainable but will also match the consumer pressure to purchase and hold environmentally conscious brands.

Transparency is one of the key measures that should exist when it comes to achieving sustainability in digital marketing. Modern consumers are now more informed and environmentally conscious about the footprints of their shopping. They want brands to be truthful regarding their sustainability practice. Thus, companies need to make their initiatives clear and genuine. This openness creates customer trust and also helps create a loyal customer base and an ethical and sustainable business.

Moreover, digital marketing can leverage data-driven strategies that will boost sustainability initiatives. Using consumer data, companies are able to understand and, advantageously, forecast ecologically friendly trends and preferences, enabling them to fit their product to these requirements. This satisfies consumers' expectations and creates a sustainable lifestyle by facilitating the use of green products and services.

Sustainability also finds its way in the digital infrastructure as sustainable practices are incorporated in the digital marketing field. Green hosting services are also on the ascending trend, where companies use renewable sources of energy to power their websites and platforms. The step not only minimizes the carbon footprint of digital operations but also sets a precedent that other businesses can emulate.

Moreover, joint ventures and cooperation are critical to the promotion of sustainability in online marketing. Together with similar organizations and NGOs, businesses can support the efforts to multiply the impact of the message about sustainability and joint actions. Such partnerships are capable of generating new solutions and campaigns that will help tackle issues that are comprehensively related to the environment.

The other tool that digital marketing has in enhancing sustainability is educational content. This is achievable because companies can empower consumers by developing and sharing knowledge on sustainability issues and motivating them to behave in a more environmentally friendly manner. This strategy serves not only to make the brand a thought leader, but also to make the consumer base better versed and responsible.

The final concern is that sustainability in digital marketing is not always a matter of reducing negative effects, but of bringing positive shifts. It demands an ecosystem where one derives sustainable practices at all nooks and crannies of the digital marketing strategy. With businesses entering the digital world, sustainability should also be perceived as an advantageous feature, as well as ethical extraction, because the number of people appreciating the protection and responsibility to the environment continues to increase.

www.ingramcontent.com/pod-product-compliance
Lightning Source LLC
Chambersburg PA
CBHW070931210326
41520CB00021B/6885